Crosscurrents / MODERN CRITIQUES
/ THIRD SERIES

Edited by Jerome Klinkowitz

Literary Subversions: New American Fiction and the Practice of Criticism
by Jerome Klinkowitz

Ronald Sukenick

IN FORM
Digressions on the Act
of Fiction

Southern Illinois University Press
CARBONDALE AND EDWARDSVILLE

For Mother, Father

Printed in the United States of America
Edited by Dan Gunter
Designed by Bob Nance, Design for Publishing, Inc.
Production supervised by Kathleen Giencke

88 87 86 85   84 4 3 2 1

Library of Congress Cataloging in Publication Data

Sukenick, Ronald.
      In form, digressions on the act of fiction.
      (Crosscurrents/modern critiques. Third series)
      1. Fiction.   I. Title.   II. Series.
PN3353.S9 1985   808.3   84–14000

ISBN 0-8093-1190-9

Contents

Crosscurrents/
Modern Critiques/
Third Series

I N THE EARLY 1960s, when the Crosscurrents/Modern Critiques series was developed by Harry T. Moore, the contemporary period was still a controversial one for scholarship. Even today the elusive sense of the present dares critics to rise above mere impressionism and to approach their subject with the same rigors of discipline expected in more traditional areas of study. As the first two series of Crosscurrents books demonstrated, critiquing contemporary culture often means that the writer must be historian, philosopher, sociologist, and bibliographer as well as literary critic, for in many cases these essential preliminary tasks are yet undone.

To the challenges that faced the initial Crosscurrents project have been added those unique to the past two decades: the disruption of conventional techniques by the great surge in innovative writing in the American 1960s just when social and political conditions were being radically transformed, the new worldwide interest in the Magic Realism of South American novelists, the startling experiments of textual and aural poetry from Europe, the emergence of Third World authors, the rising cause of feminism in life and literature, and, most dramatically, the introduction of Continental theory into the previously staid world of Anglo-American literary scholarship. These transformations demand that many traditional treatments be rethought, and part of the new responsibility for Crosscurrents will be to provide such studies.

Contributions to Crosscurrents/Modern Critiques/Third Series will be distinguished by their fresh approaches to established topics and by their opening up of new territories for discourse. When a single author is studied, we hope to present the first book on his or her work, or to explore a previously untreated aspect based on new research. Writers who have been critiqued well elsewhere will be studied in comparison with lesser-known figures, sometimes from other cultures, in an effort to broaden our base of understanding. Critical and theoretical works by leading novelists, poets, and dramatists will have a home in Crosscurrents/Modern Critiques/Third Series, as will sampler-introductions to the best in new Americanist criticism written abroad.

The excitement of contemporary studies is that all of its critical practitioners and most of their subjects are alive and working at the same time. One work influences another, bringing to the field a spirit of competition and cooperation that reaches an intensity rarely found in other disciplines. Above all, this third series of Crosscurrents/Modern Critiques will be collegial—a mutual interest in the present moment that can be shared by writer, subject, and reader alike.

Jerome Klinkowitz

Preface

WHAT FOLLOWS are the comments of a fiction writer about writing, not those of a critic on what has been written. They are more or less reports on experience—that of one engaged in an ongoing struggle with the angel of form, rather than of one studying its consequences from a cool distance: "in form," not "on form." The pieces gathered here are in fact informal, reflecting my sense that such commentary should be "invocations," as Robert Creeley says, of the creative work itself (see "Writing on Writing," pp. 226–31). The last thing I want is to burden myself with a formal theory to replace the kind of thinking that must occur in and through the creative work.

On the other hand, if there is one thing that I hope characterizes my thinking about form, it is in considering form a dynamic, rather than an inert, element of composition. In contemporary work important to me, form is not a given but an object of invention, part of the content and, like it, determined only in composition. A writer's theory is a theory of composition, rules of thumb continuous with the art, leading into it and coming out of it without claiming any privilege of authority over the poems or fictions they "invoke," and without the need to come to conclusions. This is a game in which the prize is not in concluding but in continuing. Thus my "digressions" as a form.

This is not to reduce the importance of writers writing about their art. On the contrary, such writing must take precedence over more formal criticism since it must be part of the subject of that criticism. It is pointless to resort to the Laurentian slogan about believing the writing not the writer. Criticism such as Eliot's, or for that matter, Lawrence's, is part of the writing. Further, it can be argued from the seminal effect of the best writer's criticism (Wordsworth, Coleridge, Eliot, James, Stein, etc.) that the kind of theory about composition that concerns writers has an authority beyond the theory of interpretation that concerns critics. But in a way this is not fair. Since writer's theory is continuous with writer's art, the two kinds of theory have different procedures and different ends.

Art is aimed at liberation rather than truth (see "Art and the Underground," pp. xiii–xxii), or maybe better said, at the kind of truth that makes us free. It is a way of dealing with the oppressions that stifle our consciousness, not only, in Wallace Stevens' terms, as a violence from within against a violence from without, but also against violations from within. The way an artist thinks would be scandalous for one engaged in discursive thought, and this can lead to serious misunderstandings. Stevens is a crucial figure in this respect. He is a classic case of a poet whom critics have attempted to read as if he were a philosopher. My effort is to reveal him once more as a poet (see "Wallace Stevens: Theory and Practice," pp. 157–98). An instructive example emerges of what Stevens calls "the thinking of art." Harold Bloom is right in characterizing Stevens' poetry as a process of progressive qualification rather than a search for absolute truth (see "Misreading Bloom," pp. 231–34). A writer's work is like an ongoing conversation with himself that may be overheard in a poem, a story, an essay or an interview. One can start at any point on the periphery and arrive at the center. That is the kind of unity I hoped for in putting together this volume.

Grateful acknowledgment is made to the following publications that have granted permission to reprint material originally appearing in their pages:

American Book Review (Volume 3, March–April 1981 and November–December 1981; Volume 6, January–February 1984), for "Robert Creeley," "Gerald Graff," and "Art and the Underground";

Fiction International (Numbers 2 and 3, 1974), for "Innovative Fiction/Innovative Criteria";

Lillabulero (Number 14, Spring 1974), for "Paul Metcalf: The Easy Way Out";

New Literary History (Volume 6, Winter 1974–75, and Volume 11, Spring 1979), for "Twelve Digressions Toward a Study of Composition" and "Eight Digressions on the Politics of Language";

Partisan Review (Volume 39, Fall 1972; Volume 43, Number 1, 1973; and Volume 45, Number 4, 1979) for "The New Tradition," "Thirteen Digressions," and "Misreading Harold Bloom";

SubStance (Number 27, 1980) for "The Finnegan Digression";

Studies in American Fiction (Volume 5, Spring 1977) for "Fiction in the Seventies: Ten Digressions on Ten Digressions";

Village Voice (January 25, 1973), for "Upward and Juanward."

Grateful acknowledgment is made to Alfred A. Knopf, Inc., for permission to quote from the copyright works of Wallace Stevens:

The Collected Poems of Wallace Stevens, copyright 1954 by Wallace Stevens;

The Necessary Angel, copyright 1951 by Wallace Stevens;

Opus Posthumous, copyright 1957 by Elsie Stevens and Holly Stevens.

Introduction: Art and the Underground

THE UNDERGROUND, it seems, along with corollary notions such as the avant-garde and the experimental, is an idea whose time has passed. The concept of a cultural and intellectual style in resistance to the status quo, keeping a critical distance from the establishment, and sustaining an adversary power, has been slipping out of fashion ever since Andy Warhol let us know that success is really wonderful. Artists of all kinds now understand that despite the well-advertised virtues of the garret much can be said for large, glossy lofts. Diane Wakoski points out that knocking the middle class is a little dated, especially for writers who are basically middle class. Word has come in from the intellectuals that the long rebellion of the intelligentsia against society is now over. According to Irving Howe, the last battle of the Modern movement is its losing fight to remain unsuccessful in order to maintain an adversary position. Norman Podhoretz told us long ago that ambition has replaced sex as the dirty little secret of intellectual society, and Richard Sennett has conveniently discovered that the aggressive and impersonal pursuit of self-interest is the key to a more civilized *polis*. Styles in art reflect opinion, and in writing we find a growing critical celebration of what is easily assimilated by large markets. The literati are rediscovering, with a shock of nonrecognition, what amounts to the popular style of the slick magazines of yesteryear. The democratic impulse of our literary populism matches all too well the common denominator marketing necessities of publishing conglomerates. More and more we require a literature that more and more people can understand, and the various literary strategies that encourage this tendency certainly have merit insofar as they strengthen democratic community. But we hear, through all the varied music, the ground-tone of conventional life. The last sentence is Emerson's. And it's not meant as approbation.

I quote Emerson to point out that the resistance to the conventional that we have lately called the underground is, despite the current loss of prestige for the underground and all its works, an enduring necessity for American intellectuals and, especially, for American artists. It is based on the same situation today for us as it was for Emerson in 1844 when he published his essay, "The Poet." His critique of his contemporaries as conventional did not comprise, on the other hand, an injunction to drop out and lead an extravagant, "poetic" life—though it is worth recalling that in "Self-Reliance" he advises his reader to "do your thing." The kind of unconventional life that is associated with underground or bohemian circles is acknowledged by Emerson as offering a certain freedom, but it is "the freedom of baser places," for which one pays by "dissipation and deterioration." In Emerson's conception, the poet seeks a related but superior freedom beyond the conventional that "must come from greater depth and scope of thought," and that requires in fact a way of thinking that he calls "form." Form in this sense is to be confused neither with convention nor tradition, much less with mere technique. Rather, form is a manner of thought so "passionate and alive" that it creates "an architecture of its own, and adorns nature with a new thing." Through play with form, the artist brings the sentient consciousness into contact with the wash of phenomena in new integrations that revitalize our sense of the world. This kind of thinking inescapably leads to the adversary position incorporated in the underground.

The struggle against the conventional—call it the middle class, or the bourgeoisie, or the establishment—by an adversary force going by the name of underground or bohemian or avant-garde or experimental, is the inevitable result of an American disregard for that way of thinking Emerson calls form. "The intellectual men do not believe in any essential dependence of the material world on thought and volition," Emerson maintains. We are a nation of empiricists, in which disciplines of fact overwhelm disciplines of consciousness. "Criticism is infested with a cant of materialism" that assumes the superiority of the pragmatic. Even theologians "prefer the solid ground of historical evidence," and poets, evading a more expansive and vital mode of thought, "passionate and alive," are content to sink into "a civil and conformed manner of living," and in their superficial poems fail to contact even their own experience. This failure of formal thought creates a fallout in many areas of American cultural life, prompting a frequent antagonism between art and commerce and an unfortunate schizophrenia between creativity and ordinary life. But there are also personal, ethical, and political consequences.

Even trying to come to grips with what Emerson implies by form involves thinking in new ways and asking unaccustomed questions that broach the realm practicing writers often too easily dismiss as "theoretical." It is true that what is usually meant by theory in this country is largely academic, alien to writers precisely because it employs modes of analytic thought reductive and diversionary for someome interested in writing poems and fictions. But academic theories are theories of reading and interpretation. Emerson's theories, and those of most writers including Wordsworth and Poe and Eliot and Olson and every other writer worth mentioning in this connection, are theories of composition. Thinking about composition should be continuous with formal thinking. Theories about composition—Olson's ideas about "projective verse," for example—are basically strategies that undercut the rigid vulgarities usually used to discuss writing. They should never themselves be taken too rigidly. Writers don't need theories in order to write, but they do need ways of thinking about what they do that protect their turf against the academic and the critical, and sometimes against the alien ideas of other writers. For writers overly influenced by slogans like "no ideas but in things," and "form is an extension of content," there is no point in thinking *about* writing, for it seems no more than a superior notation of phenomena and let's get on with it. But any close reading of Williams or Creeley reveals that their work is heavily involved with a dialogue between ideas and things, language and phenomena, and that part of their strength is that this dialogue is not taken for granted. A little thought may help prevent the technician of language from falling into a slipshod precision. A workshop emphasis on technique, on the well-made, evades the radically creative processes of formal thinking, disengages deep feelings, and is likely to end up being slick. Neither the accuracy of one's observation nor the polish of one's language should be the primary concern.

According to Emerson, the primary concern of the poet is liberation. First of all liberation from a mere materialism, but also liberation from the prison of ideas. Emerson is an extremist here: "Every thought is also a prison." It is not that this or that thought may be wrong or damaging or useless. *Every* thought is a prison, because a thought, once formulated, becomes an impediment to thinking. To the philosopher, to the moralist, to the critic or statesman, even to the humanist, to anyone for whom doctrine is important, such an attitude amounts to intellectual anarchy. Nevertheless, this is what Emerson is up to when he talks about form. It is a matter of valuing the process of thinking over any particular idea, even a good idea. It is on this basis that the poets are "liberating gods," why "they are free and," pun intended, "make free," why the poet "unlocks our chains." But this is also why the poet, at play in the fields of formal thinking, is regarded by the conventional citizen, the methodical thinker, the manipulating politician, as capricious, unpredictable, unreliable, and even dangerous. Artists tend to get out of control, and it is no accident that authoritarian regimes keep such tight reins on them. Plato noted the peril of poets for the state, and he was right. From the perspective of formal thinking, "nations, times, systems, enter and disappear, like threads in a tapestry of large figure and many colors," inducing a high in which we would willingly give up philosophy and religion. From the bureaucratic point of view, art is a potential threat to conformity whose production and marketing needs to be regulated like that of any other stimulant.

This condition of intellectual inebriation does not end in esthetic pleasure, but in the higher intelligence of formal perception. The freedom of formal thinking is the freedom of a state of privileged apprehension beyond pragmatic thought and "with the intellect released from all service." In freeing the processes of thought from any particular purpose, the random consciousness makes contact with the vagrant world, itself disengaged from utilitarian ends, and wins insight into the nature of mind and reality. This insight is what Emerson calls "the science of the real," and the esthetic employing it expresses the "causal and the necessary" dictated by reality. For Emerson's poet then, beauty is based on necessity: the artist's work has nothing to do with the decorative but is a strenuous investigation into the laws of reality specifically beyond the bounds of convention. The thought of the poet has "an architecture of its own," a dynamic and passionate architecture that will reflect the architecture of consciousness thinking and feeling as it processes experience. In short, form deals with the structure of experience rather than with experience itself, and in so dealing with fundamentals will be able to announce "that which no man foretold," including the poet himself. Art has an oracular function, even despite itself. In the unpredictable digression of formal thinking, the flow of the mind discovers the flow of the world and unfolds "a whole new experience." While it may hold true for other modes of thought, in formal thinking the distinction between form and content falls away, since it is the process of thought that creates the experience, which otherwise could have no prior existence.

One of the characteristics of formal thinking is that words cease to have fixed meanings. "The quality of the imagination is to flow, and not to freeze." In poetry the metamorphic power of language comes to the fore, in which alterations of meaning defamiliarize and destabilize the conventional view of reality. The vice of symbolic language is static meaning, for the point of language in poetry is to sustain connection with transformations in the self and in the world and, more important, to progressively transform the relation between self and world. A static meaning "soon becomes old and false" and in fact "all language is vehicular and transitive, and is good, as ferries and horses are, for conveyance, not as farms and houses are, for homestead." This is what Emerson calls the "algebra" of language, in which words must be considered functionally, as signs whose meanings are not fixed. "It must be abstract," as Wallace Stevens put it. Suppleness of language is necessary because formal thinking reveals the world to be in radical flux. Emerson's descriptions of it rival the transformations in a Chagall: "The mind inquires, whether these fishes under the bridge, yonder oxen in the pasture, those dogs in the yard, are immutably fishes, oxen, and dogs, or only so appear to me, and perchance to themselves appear upright men." The metamorphic power of imaginative language is a liberating force because it reveals the possibilities of experience: "Men really have got a new sense, and found within their world, another world, or nest of worlds; for the metamorphosis once seen, we divine that it does not stop."

I propose my reading of Emerson's poetic program not only because of its relevance to modern American writing—especially to poets like Ammons and Ashbery and to many of our so-called "experimental" novelists (not to mention Wallace Stevens, for whom Emerson's poetic is practically a synopsis of his own)—but to show that the anticonventional thrust of American art derives from a deep and continuing tradition intrinsic to the art itself. For if we are to believe Emerson's poetic, given the enduring conditions of American life and its prevailing business culture, there is an absolute and necessary conflict between art and the status quo.

The first priority in this situation is to encourage a way of thinking about art based on the way it is composed rather than on the way it is interpreted. Until such a mode is developed, the artist, who knows the most about his work, will al-

ways be considered by the analytic interpreter the least qualified to comment on it, and will be consigned, maybe even by
himself, to the role of an unthinking force of nature, dumb in
his way, but indulged like a child or a prize animal. Our pro-
totypical artist as dumb American is an image the French like
to promote—you supply the energy, we'll supply the brains—
though their own artists wouldn't be caught dead without a
theory. Formal thinking is profoundly nontheoretical, but
that doesn't mean it's stupid or obscurantist. I once tried to
talk W. S. Merwin into doing an article about writing and his
plausible answer was that he didn't want to spoil the mysteries. There will always be mysteries, but we should always do
our best to elevate their level by trying to understand as much
as possible. The cheap mysteries we feign, the sentimental
populism of certain poets, for example, or the know-nothing
commercialism of many novelists, are often protective poses
by which we excuse our true Emersonian purposes and iden-
tify ourselves with antiformal ways of thinking about art that
are fundamentally contemptuous of it.

Formal thinking provides a way of cogitating on creative
composition without reducing its import, but it also requires
certain admissions of intellectual dignity and civic virtue that
every writer might not be able to tolerate. Because once the
"intellectual man" in Emerson's system harnesses the imagination through formal thinking he must shoulder consider-
able public responsibility and power: "he is capable of a new
energy (as of an intellect doubled on itself), by abandonment
to the nature of things; that, beside his privacy of power as an
individual man, there is a great public power, on which he
can draw, by unlocking, at all risks, his human doors." In
comparison our "esteemed umpires of taste," or anyone who
thinks about art in a shallow way through mere comprehen-
sion of "rules and particulars," often lack not only esthetic

judgement but moral virtue. They are "persons who have acquired some knowledge of admired pictures or sculptures, and have an inclination for whatever is elegant; but if you inquire whether they are beautiful souls, and whether their own acts are like fair pictures, you learn that they are selfish and sensual." Shocking as it may seem today, imaginative power evidently requires a certain ethical impulse, not in accordance with the cheap injunctions of the boy scouts of "moral fiction," but in an obligation to the truth of things as revealed by formal thinking ("What would be base, or even obscene, to the obscene, becomes illustrious, spoken in a new connexion of thought"). But isn't it obvious that public esteem for artists, when it manifests itself, still is based on their assumed commitment to disinterested truth—with the exception, perhaps, of artists themselves, who in their skepticism of other goals sometimes assume their basic commitment is to career? As Emerson points out, "all men need to believe they live by truth." And it's up to the poet, who knows how "to utter our painful secret," to tell this kind of truth. The phony issue of "elitism" should be replaced by the real one of whether art helps the people it appeals to.

If the status quo must operate on the basis of a conventional wisdom, and especially if that wisdom has the pragmatic and quantitative basis necessary to a commercial society, then the truth of art, a disinterested truth based on other principles and without regard for the necessities of daily life, is always going to be disruptive and may at times be destructive. We live in a vigorous pragmatic culture where even the intelligentsia has little ability, sympathy, or respect for formal imaginative thinking, and where public esthetic standards rarely get beyond a false eloquence decorating a journalistic subject matter, the kind of thing august critics tend to admire on the front page of the *New York Times Book Review*. But belle letters are dead letters. In this situation the formal thinking of art is bound to be subversive. People even expect it to be subversive, and are always on the search for the easy novelty of the offbeat, but in fact the last thing most people are looking for is an art that will disrupt their lives. Art that is "passionate and alive" in Emerson's sense taps "a power transcending all limit and privacy," and is plugged into a "whole river of electricity" that is bound to transmit a shock. This is not the kind of art that is immediately pleasing. It does not titillate the conventional or "épater the bourgeoisie"; rather it makes them uncomfortable, angry, bored, and exasperated. Like Whitman, still our most Emersonian poet, its practitioner will be labeled "a fool and a churl for a long season." But we live in a society with a guilty conscience about suppressed truths whose consequences can be seen every day on the streets of any city, and there will always be much that we don't want to hear but need to know. The sign of a genuine underground is its power to provoke antagonism. If the underground seems to have lost its adversary power you can be sure that there is an underground under the underground about to make its presence felt. Because the underground is not a willed strategy but the inescapable result of an ongoing American schizophrenia between formal thinking and materialism, between art and convention and between the pragmatic and the prophetic.

1984

I. Digressions

Twelve Digressions Toward
a Study of Composition

I

Form is itself a metaphor and that of fiction is perhaps the most inclusive for our society. The form of the traditonal novel is a metaphor for a society that no longer exists. Mario Praz has described the detective story as a bourgeois fairy tale, but one could apply the description as well to the novel of social realism. Its present function is to sustain a series of comforting illusions, among which one might include the feeling that the individual is the significant focus among the phenomena of "reality" (characterization); the sense that clock, or public time is finally the reigning form of duration for consciousness (historical narration); the notion that the locus of "reality" may be determined by empirical observation (description); the conviction that the world is logical and comprehensible (causal sequence, plot). The fairy tale of the "realistic" novel whispers its assurance that the world is not mysterious, that it is predictable—if not to the characters then to the author—that it is available to manipulation by the

3

individual, that it is not only under control but that one can profit from this control. The key idea is verisimilitude: one can make an image of the real thing which, though not real, is such a persuasive likeness that it can represent our control over reality. This is the voodoo at the heart of mimetic theory that helps account for its tenacity. Though such schizoid illusions are fostered by concepts of imitation, one cannot have control "over" that of which one is part, or even formulate it completely—one can only participate more deeply in it.

II

Theory is a sign of ignorance. It becomes important when we are no longer sure what we are doing. We are passing through a time when all the "paradigms" of fiction are called into question and in consequence we begin to see the development of a poetics of fiction. Preferably the theory should be implicit in the novel, the poetics part of the poem. The perfect fiction, in this respect, would be as simple and clear as a Mozart song. However, the fact that we must now think about what we are doing may have its advantages. For one thing it may make it clear that art is on an equal footing with other intellectual disciplines; certainly it will augment the explicit scope and import of fiction. Despite the fact that there are many and disparate examples—Sterne, Fielding, Proust, Joyce—the inclusion of any kind of discursive thought in work coming out of a modern tradition overwhelmingly in favor of connotation remains problematic. One consequence is that modernist hermeticism which, at worst, leads to endless commentary about the work, dissipating its energy in abstraction, translating it into terms other than its own, or even usurping it with another text. The problem resembles that of

the physicists who discovered that the more closely they observe certain basic phenomena the more the observer becomes a factor in the observation, paradoxically obscuring
what he or she wants to observe. After a point, the more we
comment on a text the more we change it, obscure it, separate ourselves from it. The more we talk "about" a work, the
less we participate in it; the less are we engaged by the experience of it. It does no good to say that in any case literature
doesn't exist, that it is merely part of the verbal universe, the
universal discourse. This does not resolve the dilemma, it
magnifies it. For discourse itself may be "about" experience
rather than "part" of it, may be separated from experience,
like imagination from truth, form from chaos, and so on. In
fact, many modern works are, in a sense, "about" themselves—that is, they signify consciousness of themselves as
forms in process of being worked out. This is a condition of
an art whose paradigms are no longer fixed by tradition.
When consciousness of its own form is incorporated in the
dynamic structure of the text—its composition, as the painters say—theory can once again become part of the story rather than about it. One of the tasks of modern fiction, therefore, is to displace, energize, and re-embody its criticism—to
literally reunite it with our experience of the text.

III

The extreme self-consciousness of modern fiction that
seemed so aliented, schizoid, and withdrawn was in fact a critique of the contradictions of the traditional novel moving toward resolution and wholeness. The impossible situation of
the realistic novel was that the better an imitation it was of
"reality" in the Aristotelian sense, the more it was an imita-

tion in the other, Platonic sense: a shadow, a second-hand version, a counterfeit. The more intensely the novel was "about" life, the less it was part of it. The inevitably enervating conflict between art and life, imagination and reality, between thought and vitality, finally, occupies a central position in such different writers as Mann, Shklovsky, and Gide, but is most purely seen in Beckett. The head is the seat of all misery, Malone observes. This alienation of consciousness from experience is resolved in *Malone Dies* in the act of composition: the need both to comprehend and to participate in the flow of life is resolved because writing, as an act, is simultaneously part of life and about it. This formulation immediately changes the position of fiction, which can then no longer be an imitation of life but becomes, rather, an illuminating addition to its ongoing flow. Further, fiction then has to be considered not only an artifact but also an activity which brings into play its connection with the personality of the novelist, from which it was severed by, notably, Flaubert, definitively reenforced by James and Joyce. This is a great advantage since, unless you believe that the artwork produces itself—and some do believe so, though they are badly mistaken—it frees the writer to bring to bear the full resources of his experience, temperament, and intelligence without the constriction of that entirely inadequate mimetic theory which for so long has made fiction resemble a petty entertainment rather than one of the disciplines that form our consciousness. It was the genius of Henry Miller to recognize this and to employ for the first time since Rabelais (with—as far as I can recollect at the moment—the possible exception of Sterne) what might be called a free-form style of composition whose main technique is improvisation, and the great exemplar of which is jazz. At the moment, I just said, because in such a style you move from moment to moment and if you make a mistake, have a memory lapse, blow a wrong note, you either build on it anyway or leave it and do it better next time, or you lose the experiential flow. Kerouac picked this up from jazz, and so, perhaps, did the Abstract Expressionists. Art is not simply part of the universal discourse—the intelligentsia, Renato Poggioli noted, will always tend to resolve art into ideology, which, I take it, is the intelligentsia's form of Babbittry. On the contrary, it may be that that discourse is a kind of composition whose nature is best defined by art.

IV

Fiction as improvisation, all that old beatnik stuff, we've heard it before, you say, and it only opens the door to mediocrity. The door is always open to mediocrity, and no theory can close it. It is true, however, that the idea of fiction as defined by the act of composition raises formal problems that the beatniks did not even approach recognizing, much less resolve. Kerouac was simply an explosion out of the going commercial-academic complex in fiction in the direction of what was happening in the rest of the arts—in the rest of the world, for that matter. However, the work of Kerouac, taken together with that of Burroughs and of the poet-theorists with whom they are associated, should not be minimized. It represented a return to what might be called a "poetics of experience," in which art tends to be considered not about experience but part of it, and which could be argued as the most vital tradition in American writing. Since it does not feel obliged to contend with notions of transcendence inherent in a lingering religious sensibility—there is nothing sacred about poetry, noted Williams—this tradition is free to deal with experience from within rather than from without. What this implies for composition in fiction is that the writer works not from a priori ideas about what will happen and what form it will take, but in and through the text. He does not work from a presiding idea or a preexistent scenario. The next word is always a surprise. The text is generated by the activity of composition in an ongoing interchange between the mind and the page. William Burroughs made the first formal advance in American fiction given this kind of esthetic but, like the contribution of Kerouac, it was largely in terms of a break from the esthetic of the realistic novel. His "cut-up method," basically a method for developing collage relations within the text, was a way of moving from the meditated composition of the traditional novel into the unpremeditated text of what is coming to be known by Raymond Federman's term, Surfiction. This kind of fiction is best discussed in the context of the Williams-Olson idea of composition as an open field which, given the development of its conventions, Olson noted, "would be as formal as the closed, with all its traditional advantages." In fiction, and perhaps also in poetry, those formal conventions have not yet been adequately worked out.

V

"Is there anything that is not narrative?" asks Gertrude Stein in one of her lectures on narration. To speak of narration is to speak of the essential dynamic element of fiction. Fiction, as a form of invention, a way of bringing into being that which did not previously exist, is a term that can be applied to the arts in general, and perhaps to other intellectual disciplines. Narration implies time, and narrative fiction both demonstrates and partakes in the universal process by which things unfold. A little later in her lecture, in order to distinguish prose from poetry, Stein suggests that while poetry is concerned with "what," prose is concerned with "how." I would take this to mean that while poetry concerns itself with image, fiction concerns itself with process. This would seem to be borne out by the degree to which poets in the last twenty years have dropped rhythm for image as the essential element in the structure of the poem. A metaphor need have location only in space, but narrative must have location in time as well. Space plus time equals movement: things in process of happening. In a time when the center of interest in fiction has swung toward an investigation of its own essential nature, plot and story have come to seem superfluous elements of the art. The essential story that fiction tells is that of motion and stasis, and it would seem that whatever the particular terms of this process, or whatever its level of occurrence—narrative, story, plot, incident—without it we are dealing with some other art. The fiction that poets write, while often admirable for image, structure, and beauty of statement, is just as often unbearably static. The spatialization of time that has been an important development in modern fiction, as Sharon Spencer demonstrates, has not been a tendency toward stasis, but an effort to fix the space of the page as the location of movement in narration, rather than the illusionary space of "reality" as in the mimetic novel. The collapse of illusionary time in realistic fiction parallels the collapse of illusionary space in perspective painting and serves a parallel function: the assertion of the validity of the work of art in its own right rather than as an imitation of something else.

VI

Just as one cannot say that a piece of music is "about" its melody, one should not say that a piece of fiction is "about" its subject matter—subject matter is just one element of the composition. When we consider a novel, or any other artwork, we are considering an artifact, and to deal with it as if it were merely another way of conveying information about something else is to accept the terms of discussion set by mimetic fiction. A novel conveys information about itself. We would not think of calling a Bach fugue self-conscious because it is not program music—or even speak of it as "about itself" for that matter. That we have to resort to such terms testifies to our impoverished vocabulary concerning the most fundamental elements of fiction. A person can be self-conscious, an artifact cannot. Even the most involved confessions of Narcissus himself are merely grist for the mill, the subconscious caught up in a discourse of consciousness, consciousness of self caught up in the novelist's consciousness of the artifact he is fabricating. From the point of view of composition, a novel is a developing structure that from the first word has its own influence in determining its shape, and by the last has far more influence than its author. A generative theory of fiction would consider the novel from the point of view of composition, just as music theory is essentially the theory of composition, just as that of any art not distracted by incidental effects of mimesis would be the theory of composition. But, you object, the literary arts, unlike the others, employ words that signify referents beyond the works themselves. The context of the art work always changes what it includes. The words used meditatively in a literary work are not the same words used instrumentally in the world of action. Words in dreams do not mean the same thing as words in the newspaper. The word *fog* in *Bleak House* does not mean the same thing as the word *fog* in the dictionary, though its meaning in *Bleak House*, once developed, could be, probably has been, added to the general sense—one sees this process on any page of the OED. What language signifies in a literary work is different from what it signifies in its general sense, but then may be added to that sense.

VII

Language is a self-contained system. Oui, monsieur. But the art of fiction and poetry lies precisely in opening that system up to experience beyond language. The obligation of fiction is to rescue experience from history, from politics, from commerce, from theory, even from language itself—from any system, in fact, that threatens to distort, devitalize, or manipulate experience. The health of language depends on its contact with experience, which it both embodies and helps to create. The question is, "How can art open itself maximally to experience without destroying its integrity as artifact?" The Duchamp idea of an art context seems to me a big mistake. The art context is not simply a concept, but is exactly what is to be made by the artist, is the work of art itself. Merely placing a shovel in the art field, however you might want to define that field, does not make the shovel a work of art. This would be the equivalent, for fiction, of claiming that subject matter can make a novel. If that were true, then the new journalists would be justified in claiming that depth reportage is the new fiction. The art field is a nexus of various kinds of energy, image, and experience. What they are, and how they interact, may in the long run be the most profitable area for criticism: the study of composition.

VIII

It is not that art does not exist but that it does not preexist. That is to say, it cannot be defined. Since it works at the interface of system and disorder, form and chaos, meaning and meaninglessness, it must by nature constantly define and dedefine itself. One might even consider every successful work of art a unique definition—a definition of itself. Such a definition cannot be generalized; on the contrary, it tends to call into question the other works in its genre. The criticism that a work of art lacks definition is far more serious than that it lacks beauty: a work can succeed on a variety of grounds other than beauty, but if it fails to distinguish itself as a unique entity it cannot succeed on any grounds. Questions on the order of "what is fiction?" are, therefore, not likely to be very fruitful. If fiction may be considered an activity, however, it does make sense to talk about what that activity is and how it generates the work. Such discussion may provide at least a running definition—one always running to keep up with the development of the art. As an activity, fiction first of all involves a flow of energy. This is a factor that seems insufficiently recognized and it might be interesting to reconsider the novel in its terms. The flow of energy in Henry Miller or in Rabelais is broad and direct, while that in Hemingway is constricted almost to the point of stoppage. *Clarissa* is filled with the heat of repressed energy, *Wuthering Heights* with the released energy of dreams. The quality of energy in Henry James is schizoid in its disembodied consciousness and in this resembles, surprisingly, Beckett. In some examples of nouveau and nouveau nouveau roman, energy seems withdrawn almost to the point of catatonia—an effect that may be desired as part of an effort to cancel the imprint of personality. Though there is not necessarily plot or story in a narrative, there is always a field of action, and in a field of action the way energy moves should be the most obvious element.

IX

The narrative is a field of action, a context that will modify whatever enters it. The man walking from the bench onto the football field becomes an entity in a game, subject to its rules and interactions. Everything takes on a different significance. Rain for the spectator means that he will get wet, for the player that the field will be muddy. The game exists independently of "real life," though it is also part of it. But though narrative resembles a game, it is not a game; or, rather, the game is what is being made up, the context that will become *Moby-Dick* or *Pride and Prejudice*, never twice the same.

X

In a generative theory, formally, narrative would be the movement of the mind as it organizes the open field of the text. In a vitalistic sense, it would be the energy of personality reversing the entropy of experience—also known as "subject matter," or "content"—as it enters the field of the text. The result is a new experience, distinguished by the way it salvages energy from that constant dissipation characteristic of the flux. Part of the field consists of the structure of language, the norms inherent in it, the dictates imposed by it, the knowledge preserved through it. Part consists of the texture of the culture, and part, more specifically, of the literary tradition. Part also consists of particularized incident. These, and undoubtedly many other elements, rest inert until, one might say, the current of personality, of a particular temperament, begins to flow through them, organizing things in the way it characteristically tends to organize them. And as the field becomes organized, the shaping influence of personality, and of any other single element, becomes less and less until finally it is the structured field itself that becomes the organizing power, shaping personality, shaping energy, shaping language, culture, literary tradition.

XI

An essentialized narrative is still at the heart of fiction—it embodies the progression of the mind as it confronts and affects experience. Such a formulation would cover such apparently antinarrative modes of organization as collage linkage. From the point of view of causal sequence, the kind of sequence developed by linkage of disparate fragments might seem lunatic, but it might be argued that this kind of organization is one of the mind's most formidable methods of organizing the disparities of experience. It has the virtue of generating unforeseen connections, and is particularly useful in a time when traditional causes no longer seem adequate to account for observed effects. It may produce new systems of order when traditional ones no longer seem persuasive. Since it starts beyond system it is capable of including kinds of experience that given systems might exclude. Or if such a method of organization is considered as a system, then it is an open system. The idea of collage linkage implies discontinuity and the value of the collage fragment in itself, beyond any system. Causal narrative implies continuity and wholeness, but with the constant threat of discontinuity and fragmentation. Non-causal narrative implies discontinuity and fragmentation reaching toward continuity and wholeness, which seems more appropriate to a time when mystiques and their processes are laid bare.

XII

The blank page, the void where everything is called into question.

1974

Thirteen Digressions

I

When LeRoi Jones [Baraka] introduced his 1963 anthology of contemporary fiction, *The Moderns*, by claiming descent from the modern tradition for "the best of American twentieth century writing," it seemed to me an unquestionable premise. But now it seems clear there has been a break in that descent, and that to make it explicit and disentangle ourselves from some of the tendencies of modernism, and especially from its attendant criticism, will clear the air. There have been unforeseen, though maybe predictable, developments. The hermeticism of the moderns engendered, not without their implicit and, at times, explicit encouragement, a new and reductive academicism. The New Criticism, with its ideas about hypostasis, intentional fallacy, ambiguity, and withheld emotion, emphasized the hermetic side of the moderns and attenuated the poem's connection with experience. One must sustain tension rather than achieve catharsis. Irony, highly valued as a means of control, becomes a form of suppression that chokes off libido. The hermeneutics of the New Criticism was, in part, a prophylaxis designed to protect life from the disruptive energy of art. If art is potential disease (disorder, plotlessness, idiosyncratic form, irregular versification), it follows that interpretation must be quarantine. It was in reaction to this kind of devitalization that Sontag demanded an erotics of art.

II

There was another and opposite side to the American moderns that may turn out to be the most important and most native aspect of their work, though it was not picked up by the critics descending from Eliot (who now begins to seem an isolated, exceptional figure among the rest) since it contradicts their image of literature which tended toward that of a closed box. I am referring to the continuity of art and experience that is so obvious in *The Cantos* and in the work of Williams, especially *Paterson*. It is evident in the readiness of these poets to use their own unmediated experience without the intervention of predetermined form, including the experience that occurs during and because of composition, on the same level as other subject matter. In Wallace Stevens one might say that this latter experience is the poem: that the poem is experience mediated only by the further experience of composition, the famous "act of the mind." This is why Stevens is confusing for amateur philosophers, who think he is seriously formulating abstractions, when he is in fact doing something more playful and far more serious—showing us how abstractions operate in experience, how they transmute, how they contradict one another, how they repeat and vary and interact with other kinds of experience, how they feel.

Pound speaks of a "persona." All right. Maybe he still felt
the need to fictionalize his experience as, say, Browning
might in order to incorporate it into the artifice of the poem.
Nevertheless, the way that Pound and Williams incorporate
personal anecdotes, for example, even letters, is something
new. The poem is continuous with speech, with conversation, with thought, with experience, and is not a special category—except in one respect: there is an additional variable,
the process of the composition of the poem, which, however,
is itself continuous with experience.

III

It was this essentially "Redskin" attitude toward experience
in a new and explict form that blew the lid off the closed and
stuffy art of the fifties and released a flood of energy in a
whole generation of creative artists. The improvisations of
jazz, especially bebop, were the great example, explicitly so
in Kerouac's "Essentials of Spontaneous Prose." There was
Olson's 1950 "Projective Verse" essay: "It is now only a
matter of the recognition of the conventions of composition
by field for us to bring into bcing an open verse as formal as
the closed, with all its traditional advantages." The first real
explosion was Abstract Expressionism, which obliterated the
demarcation between the painting and the experience of
composing it. There was Frank O'Hara, whose poems are
like casual notations of what happens as he goes along in a casual diction and flattened metric that reads quite differently
from what one was used to thinking of as poetry. There was
John Cage and his ideas about open-ended, chance composition, which have had enduring influence (the artist Robert
Morris in 1970: "the artist has stepped aside for more of the

world to enter into the art"). There was Allen Ginsberg's exploitation of his own personality in his poems. There were Jack Spicer and Robert Duncan on the West Coast. In the novel there were Kerouac and Burroughs. And there were many others. A poet as different from the preceding figures as A. R. Ammons is very much like them with respect to his use of experience, especially in his book-length poem *A Tape for the Turn of the Year*. Poetic closure became relatively unimportant. Letters, journals, and collaborations became important forms. Tape recording became a significant technique in various arts—I remember the composer Steve Reich telling me the tape recorder was the characteristic medium of the decade. Improvisation was crucial (Kerouac: "Begin not from preconceived idea of what to say about image but from jewel center of interest in subject of image at moment of writing"). Like improvisation, collage was also crucial as a way of making fresh contact with experience. There was a more direct relation with experience as it registers on the self without the mediation of a priori form, and a correspondingly increased importance of the presence of the self in the work. One felt the need to incorporate the vagaries of experience, its randomness, its arbitrariness, to affirm the experience of composition, and to deny the work as illusion, so that while we admitted the brokenness, the discontinuity of experience, we also swept away many of the chronic schizoid Western attitudes toward mind and experience, thought and poetry, form and chaos, and we gave to our works the only structure that seemed possible or even desirable—the structure of our own minds.

If another kind of structure seemed possible, it was the structure of the arbitrary, a way of moving from the meditated to the unpremeditated, as in Burrough's "cut up" method, of allowing "more of the world to enter into the art" (one notes already in Stevens this alternation between arbitrary forms and forms that reflect the dynamic of his ongoing imagination). Diane Wakoski, one of the important poets in this line, recently made the following comment on this esthetic, which I quote while taking exception to her organic/life style:invention/craft opposition and her comment on fiction:

Those of us writing poetry today are doing so on a series of formal premises which may be different from anything in the past. One of those premises is that the work must organically come out of the writer's life. We do not believe very much in "invented" literature any more. Or we consider it entertainment. Neither serious nor interesting art. We have some difficulty dealing with the idea that a man could sit down and decide to write, say, a sonnet or a villanelle and turn out a poem that would really be interesting to anyone. Even technically or perhaps especially technically, because what we are interested in is how the writer reaches through the content of his life, his ideas, his emotions, and his own personality to create a form for expressing all of this. . . . We no longer accept the premise that a novelist can invent people or stories without putting himself into them. We no longer believe that there is something called "the craft of poetry" which is apart from the life style of the poet. . . . I'd like to . . . make a case for the excitement in literature being an extension of the writer's life, rather than a transcending of or an escape from his reality.

Extension rather than transcendence. If we say that "content" is the writer's experience (memories, researches, readings, activities, indigestions, imaginings, neuroses, opinions, and the act of composition), then Wakoski's commentary makes perfect sense of Creeley's formulation that "form is an extension of content." The poem is not different from experience, it is more experience. If this is so then we can and should talk about poetry more like the way we talk about baseball than the way we talk about God. It might then be seen as the duty of interpretation to avoid hierophantic complications and to render itself unnecessary as it extends our experience of the poem.

IV

It's possible that a break with what was considered literary modernism occurred in the fifties without anyone being quite aware of it, even the writers themselves (in painting, the disruption was more explicit). Maybe the significant split on hermeticism was between Eliot and Pound on one side and Williams and Stevens (literally) on the other, though the split is more or less embodied in all these figures. The break is implicit in the distinction Olson made between Pound and Williams in the *Mayan Letters* of 1953, but this is apparently not what Olson thought he was saying: "The primary contrast, for our purposes is, BILL: his Pat is the exact opposite of Ez's, that is, Bill HAS an emotional system which is capable of extensions & comprehensions the ego-system (the Old Deal, Ez as Cento Man here dates) is not." In 1965, Creeley, to whom the *Letters* were written, glossed this to mean that, for Pound, "the ego or mind is made the sole measure of such experience" while "Williams offers an emotional system, which does not limit the context of writing to an assumption of understanding." It seems to me that the real difference in question is simply that between an imposed order and one that develops as it goes along—"occurs as it occurs," as Stevens would say, "by digression" as Laurence Sterne would put it, or, in terms of jazz, by improvisation. If it is true that such a way of proceeding is capable of comprehensions beyond those of the "ego-system," it may be to say that art is a way of thinking that is different from and in many ways superior to abstract thinking. In any case, it is true more often than not that, in retrospect, revolutionaries revolutionize something other than what they thought they did. For example, the attempts of Williams and Olson to explain their metric never makes sense to me unless I think of them as an unrecognized transition from verse that is largely oral to verse that is largely visual ("concrete")—the opposite of what they are saying.

V

Though I am not concerned here with literary theory, I must stress the importance of the kind of working theory that influences the process of composition. There are three theories that, in modern history, have generally governed what an artist, consciously or nonconsciously, thinks he is doing in his work: roughly in order of their appearance—though they are also obviously coexistent—they are imitation, expression, illumination. There is also a fourth idea of composition which is beginning to crystallize and to dominate the work of artists who are in touch with their contemporaneity, that I will call generation. The relation of these theories is not successive but metabolic: each digests the preceding way of organizing things into its own particular way of organizing things. Imitation is the most pervasive and most deeply embedded theory of art in our culture (though in many others it is not), particularly for the novel. It's hard to avoid. Let's take the example of two good novelists (the comments of whom I consider here, I want to add, do not necessarily reflect their creative practice). William Gass talks about fiction as an addition to reality, and Gilbert Sorrentino talks about fiction as invention. Both of these terms I would characterize as having to do with art as generation, but both writers seem at the same time encumbered in their thinking by undigested leftovers from other theories. Gass thinks of fiction as a model of the world—an idea itself modeled, probably, on the abstract schemes of reality developed in the exact sciences. But the idea of a model reintroduces the schizoid split between art and reality that one gets rid of in speaking about art as an addition to reality (as Gass does elsewhere). A model is a model of something else that is "real." A model is not real. The real is the subject of the model. The model is the form we give to the subject. This is basically a subtler kind of imitation theory in which continuity between art and experience is broken because art is seen as a mode essentially different from experience. One of the consequences of such theories is the distinction between form and content: form is justifiably seen as merely a way for formulating content, rather than as the creation of content, that is, as addition to reality. Another consequence is a literature that cannot believe in its own reality and must have constant recourse to irony and self-parody, a literature that has lost confidence in itself: Barth's "literature of exhaustion," or what critic Jerome Klinkowitz calls "regressive parody." Still another consequence is the desperate reintroduction of realism as media realism, stereotype: Pop Art. As if the only thing we can make of our experience is the ultimate mirror image—a photograph, a negative, a cliché.

VI

Gilbert Sorrentino, in his essay on Williams's prose in *New American Review* 15, strongly rejects the mimetic theory for the novel. "It does not mirror reality," he concludes of the novel.

But then he immediately adds: "If it is any good at all it mirrors the processes of the real, but, being selective, makes a form that allows us to see these processes with clarity." This I see as still another variant of the idea of imitation, and in fact I think it could be argued that this version is probably much what Aristotle had in mind to begin with. Sorrentino also rejects fiction as "the expression of 'self,' " and here, with some qualification, I would agree with him. The use of the self was an important element in the kind of literature of experience that was prominent in the sixties. However, this should not be confused with that distorted scrap of the romantic tradition, commonly called "self-expression." The use of the self in such books as Steve Katz's *Exagggerations of Peter Prince* and my own *Up* was quite contrary to the doctrine of self-expression. We were not writing autobiography or confession—we were at times using those forms as ways of incorporating our experience into fiction at the same level as any other data. To quote Diane Wakoski again, this time in an interview: "I use personal information about my life in the same way that anyone else who had a complicated body of knowledge might use it, as a structure or metaphor, a set of images for poetry." Possibly a more important reason for using one's experience at the same level as other data was to break down the rather puritan conception of art as illusion, which, in a crude sense, is made necessary by mimetic theory (if art isn't real it must be illusion). It's a telling fact that the idea of art as realism can't do without the idea of art as illusion. Art as illusion is fundamentally a negative characterization which must then be circumvented by such awkward detours as the willing suspension of disbelief, which seems an adequate theory for children reading fairy tales but not for much else. In order to help break down the "willing suspension of disbelief" I threw in the notion of "the truth of the page." In an interview done in 1969 (published 1971) I am recorded as follows:

> The truth of the page is that there's a writer sitting there writing the page. There's a dictum of Burroughs which goes something like "the writer shouldn't be writing anything except what's in his mind at the moment of writing," which means to me the same thing as "the truth of the page." . . . I'm not writing illusions—I'm not writing about a fantasy that I've had, if it's fantasy, but I'm having a fantasy and writing it down. In fact, the act of writing it down is part of the fantasy . . . like sleeping is part of dreaming.

If the writer is conceived, both by himself and by the reader, as "someone sitting there writing the page," illusionism becomes impossible and several advantages are gained. First, one comes closer to the truth of the situation. Second, for the writer, writing becomes continuous with the rest of his experience. Third, the writer is clearly at liberty to use whatever material comes into his head as he is writing, including the data of his own experience. Fourth, he becomes, in Wordsworth's phrase, "a man speaking to men," and therefore continuous with their experience. Fifth, the reader is prevented from being hypnotized by the illusion of that make-believe so effective in the hands of nineteenth-century novelists but which by now has become a passive, escapist habit of response to a creative work—instead he is forced to recognize the reality of the reading situation as the writer points to the reality of the writing situation, and the work, instead of allowing him to escape the truth of his own life, keeps returning him to it but, one hopes, with his own imagination activated and revitalized. To paraphrase Robbe-Grillet, the main didactic job of the contemporary novel is to teach the reader now to imagine his own life. Art is not imitation; it is example.

VII

Henry Miller is for American novelists what Whitman is for American poets. The source of his vitality is the current that began flowing when he reconnected our art with our experience. Experience begins with the self and Miller put the self back into fiction. For a writer the whole point of literary technique is the fullest possible release of the energy of the personality into the work, and when one comes into contact with that force, the whole superstructure that one had assumed to be the point of literature begins to burn away. After Miller it was possible to gather strength from Sterne, Rabelais, Beckett—the latter's reduction of the self to the most irreducible minimum can be seen as the complementary opposite of Miller's tendency to magnification. Watt's cryptic word games that treat language as detached, autonomous, hermetic, and that can be read as a parody of Joyce, indicate a literary difference between the friends. For Beckett, however autonomous language may be, it is finally the last sign of the presence of identity and, if only through the act of composition, of a vestigial, irreducible, and perhaps undesirable connection with experience. In his hermeticism, Joyce is modern; Beckett is the beginning of something else. Another way of seeing the reintroduction of the self in fiction is as an element of expressive theory, an aspect of romantic theory. In an expressive theory I take it that what is being expressed is not the self but a relation—that is, the self becomes important as a term in relation with another term: nature in *The Prelude*, for example. The second term has to do with some conception of reality, and the imagination becomes the means of uniting the self with reality. However, this works only if there are two terms to unite, and it may be that the hermeticism of the moderns had to do with the loss of the second term. I suspect that for most contemporary artists (I mean artists who are aware of their contemporaneity) there is no conception of reality strong enough to prevent an expressive approach from lapsing into solipsism. Genet's brilliance was in sensing that the imagination could no longer unite us with reality unless it invented it to begin with.

VIII

In a situation where the notion of reality is itself up in the air, a theory of art that has to do with the illumination of reality will be seen to have obvious deficiencies. Again, Sorrentino, in his highly intelligent Williams essay, augments what is basically a mimetic theory with the theory of illumination. The novel not only "mirrors the processes of the real" but also shows us its essence, reveals its "actuality." In other words, the novel does not merely imitate, it illuminates: "the flash, the instant or cluster of meaning"—illuminating what? For many of us writing now the flash of insight reveals the void. The only kind of epiphany that can occur in the absence of a second term would be a negative epiphany. The symbolists had various conceptions of the absolute available through correspondences, and the surrealists had the unconscious via depth imagery, but generally speaking the notion of illumination seems like a doomed effort by the remnants of religious sensibility to find meaning in a secularized reality. No wonder that Narcissus was a compelling figure for the symbolists and their descendants. In such circumstances what the lamp reveals is the mirror—or nothingness, le Neant. Even for Joyce epiphany becomes inadequate as first social reality, then culture, as second terms, dissolve in language in *Finnegans Wake*. Still, it seems to me that the idea of illumination has a certain kind of validity—as long as it is clear that revelation does not come from some source beyond ourselves, some essence that enables us to transcend our present state. It may be that the mind at its most illumined confronting the world at its most obscure is able to generate extensions of experience that alter and unify the field of experience itself.

IX

" 'Nature does not use *pi*' means that nature does not measure bubbles but generates them." Hugh Kenner's interpretation of Buckminster Fuller's remark (in *The Pound Era*) is wholly in the line of the open field idea of composition articulated by Williams and Olson, and within the realm of what I have called a generative theory of composition. "*Pi* will only describe a sphere once formed, and a sphere moreover idealized because static. But the generation of forms is described by vectors." To take off from there, let's say that *pi* is the point of view of art as static and measureable, as in Aristotle: form is a description of forms that already exist, and that may be transferred to works that do not yet exist. Thus, metrical scansion, traditional forms, the well-made novel. In an open field, or generative, theory of composition, the page would be a field of forces whose vectors generate the poem. There is no a priori form—form is generated by the currents of energy that interact on the page. Robbe-Grillet has spoken about the question of generation in composition, but I prefer a modification of his ideas suggested by Ricardou: "It is the activity of writing which provokes the activity of invention in presenting it with problems, in imposing directions on it, in endlessly pushing it ahead. It is in and through the text that the text is produced." This resembles that art of the sixties in which the mechanics of the medium produced the work, without, however, its naive ambition to substitute process for artist. In this view, the page would become a model, or better, record—not of "reality"—but of the way the mind works, the way we experience things, including the way we experience creative thought. "Mind is the regenerative part of nature," Kenner remarks further on. And, one might add, art is the regenerative part of experience as it generates new antientropic extensions of it that reestablish a vital connection with the data of reality in the energy field of the art work. That's why we can say that art makes life more real.

X

If art is not reflection of reality then the last reflection to get rid of in self reflection. The fate of Narcissus is to drown in contemplation of himself. The way out of the dilemma of Narcissus lies in the work of art as artifice. As artifice the work of art is a conscious tautology in which there is always an implicit (and sometimes explicit) reference to its own nature as artifact—self-reflexive, not self-reflective. It is not an imitation but a new thing in its own right, an invention. The very fact that it has validity only within its own terms is what cuts it loose from the solipsism of Narcissus. The successful work of art is a discrete energy system that takes its place among the other things of our world, available to the experience of anyone who is interested. Perhaps that is why the art critic, Jack Burnham, speaking of a contemporary artist, remarks that the problem he addresses is "how can sculpture define itself most rigorously as tautology." Instead of hiding its tautological nature with illusion, contemporary art capitalizes on it. This was a point that was made well and often in the art of the sixties: one immediately thinks of the precedents of Fellini, Genet, Beckett, and behind them the precedents of Brecht, Shklovsky, Sterne.

XI

Among other things, full recognition of the art work as artifice rather than illusion means full recognition of the two realities behind literature: the reality of the spoken word and the reality of the written word. On one hand we get a resurgence of poetry as speech, Allen Ginsberg, the importance of the tape recorder, poetry as song lyric; and on the other hand, concrete poetry, the importance of arrangement on the page rather than traditional metric and, for the novel, no longer leaving one of the most important elements of composition in the hands of the typesetter: the placement of print on the page becomes an expressive resource of the novel. On one hand we get forms that have to do with time—the time it takes to compose the work or to experience it—that emphasize the process of composition and make it an important, often the most important, expressive element; and on the other hand we get an arbitrary formalism that has to do with space—a decision to arrange all lines and larger segments in groups of three, for example.

One of the curious effects of a shift from art as illusion to art as artifact, and an example of how a new theory of composition subsumes rather than obliterates its predecessors, is the fate of description in fiction. Since it is no longer the novelist's business to "make us see" as it was in terms of imitation theories, description in fiction would seem to be pointless, but this is not the case. Description is too deeply embedded in the tradition of the novel ever to be lost, but its present significance is ironically antithetical to its former one. The con-

temporary novelist describes things with whose appearance
we are already perfectly familiar (through photography, film,
travel, or simply the modern quotidian) not to make us see
those things but to test the language against them, to keep it
alive to visual experience. The pleasure of description is the
pleasure of a linguistic skill, not that of a genre painting.

XII

Maintaining that an artwork is true only within its own terms
opens it to a description as a beneficial form of counterfeit,
forgery, fraud, or lie. This argument is often urged with regard to fiction. Fiction is neither true nor false factually, but
only good and bad. One might say that its truth is poetic
truth: a statement of a particular rapport with reality sufficiently persuasive that we may for a time share it. This kind
of "truth" does not depend on accurate description of "reality" but rather itself generates what we call reality, reordering
our perceptions and sustaining a vital connection with the
world, and may be considered on a parity with truth generated in other disciplines that extend, reorder, and vitalize the
human domain. It works against schizoid withdrawal into
abstraction or solipsism, and at the same time works against
entrapment in its own tautologies by constantly dissolving
them in experience. The Word makes the world a poem, then
becomes irrelevant. Even so enlightened a novelist as Raymond Federman, who, however, still harbors a French structuralist orientation toward language, speaks in his essay
"Surfiction" of the necessary "fraudulence" of the novel. He
quotes my letter in reply in his anthology, *Surfiction*:

Rather than serving as a mirror or redoubling on itself, fiction adds
itself to the world, creating a meaningful "reality" that did not pre-

viously exist. Fiction is artifice but not artificial. It seems as pointless to call the creative powers of the mind "fraudulent" as it would
be to call the procreative powers of the body such. What we bring
into the world is *per se* beyond language, and at that point language
is of course left behind—but it is the function of creative language
to be left behind, to leave itself behind, in just that way. The word is
unnecessary once it is spoken, but it has to be spoken. Meaning
does not pre-exist creation and afterward it may be superfluous.

Such writing progressively works against itself in order to
move us beyond language back into other aspects of experience. The wisdom of creative language includes the sense of
its own limitations. But one must not lose sight of its power:
creative writers deal with the enormous knowledge inherent
in language and do not need the truths of discursive communication as an excuse for their art.

XIII

Since we live in fictions, the job of the novelist is the almost
impossible one of specifically not writing fiction, of unwriting
novels—through our particular excellence creating books
that suddenly, as we look over our shoulders, we realize have
become, inevitably, novels. We are in a totally different position from those moderns who were trying to transcend the
real in isolated and unique visions. Instead, we are trying to
plunge through literature into the world and commonalty
(though on our own terms—the terms created in our novels).
Our yen is union, not separation—to break through those
cheap or outlived fictions which separate us from our world.
The question is not the validity of this or that kind of fiction,
but of the fictive process itself, which, far more than a literary
matter, involves belief, myth, and the ways we understand
experience. We live in language, and only writers are free—

only they know how to move into a more and more spacious syntax. The moderns questioned the idea of a priori form; we question the idea of form itself. The innovative fiction writers of the American sixties were still writing "novels" even though they understood that "the" novel as defined at that time in this country—quite provincially, it is necessary to add—was a form whose credibility was exhausted. We write beyond any definitions of form because we believe that fiction is always in process of defining itself. Not the form but the imaginative process that creates the form is exemplary. Form is the embodiment, the temporary context of the imagination, an embodiment that is the consequence of the questioning of form by the imagination. For the fiction of the seventies, this point of view resulted in a proliferation and variety of formal options. At the same time, the formal opening out of the sixties has raised the problem of how a work can remain continuous with experience while sustaining an internal structure that distinguishes it from other areas of experience. The slackness and characterlessness of much recent poetry that still bears the mark of the art of the sixties is the result of its failure to confront this problem. What Raymond Federman calls Surficton has been essentially an exploration of the formal geometry of the open field by the imagination which, in so engaging it, generates the unpredictable text. The future novel, says Federman, will be "a kind of discourse whose shape will be an interrogation, an endless interrogation of what it is doing while it is doing it." In a world that pushes constantly in the direction of the impersonal and systematic we need fiction (and criticism) that is subversively personal and unsystematic—Miller, Sterne, Rabelais—unruly, unpredictable, threatening to humanists with its humanness.

1976

Fiction in the Seventies:
Ten Digressions on Ten Digressions

The history of American fiction since the fifties has been a mistake. From the vantage of the seventies, it would seem that the novel, in part along with the other arts, has been involved in a variety of fallacies the pursuit of which it can no longer afford to sustain. Every movement must have its heresies, and the movement of fiction through the seventies is no exception. However, instead of listing a series of Fallacies, I would like to discuss a number of Digressions. A Digression implies a wrong-headed though possibly interesting detour that may return one to the Path all the wiser. Let me begin with a few sweeping generalizations in full consciousness that sweeping generalizations are never the truth; but then, what is truth when it comes to fiction? I am assuming that Bellow and Malamud represent the ficton of the fifties, and it is still a very fine kind of fiction, at its best, as almost any kind of fiction is very fine at its best. The fiction of the sixties would be Barth, Barthelme, Pynchon, Brautigan and so on, that is, those innovators who are now well-known but not yet elder statesmen, who are considered, and in the strict sense are, "contemporary." Fiction writers who seem to represent something particular about the current decade, therefore, have been referred to as post-contemporary: George Chambers, Raymond Federman, Eugene Wildman, Jerry Bumpus, Ishmael Reed, Harry Matthews, Clarence Major, Steve Katz, Michael Brownstein, Jon Baumbach, Russell Banks, and Robert Coover, among many others.

I. The Parodic Digression

Fiction in the fifties was august and self-confident—not for any good reason, it just was. The novel was still the great symphonic form in the world of letters. There was the tradition of the "great novel." Ficton thought of itself as evolving periodically into imposing masterpieces that would justify the form. The important thing about *Ulysses* was not that it called into question the very fictive tradition it epitomized, but that it was a "great novel," one in a series. Only that could explain the awe in which it was held and the totality with which it was ignored by fiction in the fifties. Fiction at that time paid a great deal of lip service to Joyce, Kafka, Lawrence, Proust, Faulkner, and literary modernism, but somehow all that had very little to do with us, with fiction in America, it can't happen here. Nevertheless, fiction was not completely comfortable with itself as it moved through the sixties. It began to manifest an uneasiness, an odd guilt, a certain confusion. Eminent novelists like Philip Roth and John Barth began to tell us that fiction was no longer possible, that it was at the end of its rope. What was so-called "black humor" again, it's hard to remember? In a recent article on the subject, subtitled "Fiction in the Sixties," Morris Dickstein reminds us:

We must distinguish between verbal black humorists, such as Terry Southern, Bruce Jay Friedman, and even Philip Roth, whose basic

unit is the sick joke or the stand-up monologue, and what I would
call "structural" black humorists, such as Heller, Pynchon and
Vonnegut. The former take apart the well-made novel and substitute nothing but the absurdist joke, the formless tirade, the cry in
the dark; the latter tend toward overarticulated forms, insanely
comprehensive plots. . . . Both kinds of black humorists are making an intense assertion of self—the former directly, the latter in
vast structures of self-projection.[1]

Black humor, in both of its manifestations, indicated a loss of
faith in the conventional forms of the novel, and an assertion
of the identity, or at least the hand, of the novelist. The inevitable consequence was *The Parodic Digression*. These were
novels by novelists who no longer believed in THE novel but
felt compelled for one reason or another to write it. The literature of exhaustion, the death of the novel. One critic has
labelled the novelists who became well-known in the late sixties as "regressive parodists"—regressive because fiction at
that time stubbornly refused to let go of its last superstition,
that it is "about" something, that it is mimetic, that it can be
validated on the grounds that it presents a superior vision of
"reality," finer and deeper than that of history, journalism,
or TV. If fiction couldn't do that, what then could it do? How
could it compete with the daily newspaper? It couldn't, said
Tom Wolfe. And for a while fiction believed him, in the guise
of Norman Mailer and Truman Capote, among others.

II. The Journalistic Digression

Fiction is a kind of deep reportage. Thus novelists will be
truest to their art if they become super-journalists, and re-
porters using the techniques of fiction are in a position to
usurp the novel. Fiction is not a kind of reportage. Those

who believe this mistake one phase in the novel's development—realism—for the nature of fiction, though it must be
said that this has been a chronic mistake even among those in
the critical establishment favorable to fiction, who now reap
what they have sown. The novel has always been connected
with reportage but the two are not the same. *Moll Flanders* was
supposed to be the inside dope on a prostitute and *Jonathan
Wild* capitalized on "the true history" of that crook. In other
words, fiction may pretend to be reportage, and vice versa,
but they are two different things. One is of course also aware
of all the phases in the development of the novel that have
nothing to do with social realism, from Rabelais to *Finnegans
Wake*, from Choderlos de Laclos to late Henry James, romance, allegory, psychological analysis, the novel of sensibility, Diderot, Sterne, Gothic, *Wuthering Heights*, the whole
modern novel, etc., etc. The point is that journalism is of necessity after the fact, it is a report about something that has
happened; creative writing is the fact—before the act of writing there was no fact—that's why it's creative. *Wuthering
Heights* is itself fact: a culture fact, an artifact. It is not about
some other fact. *Electric Kool-Aid Acid Test* is about Ken Kesey; *Wuthering Heights* is about *Wuthering Heights*. "But it's also
about the moors, a certain region in England, about Heath-
cliff, about the English family . . ." Yes, that's right. It's
about *Wuthering Heights*. Nevertheless, *The Journalistic Digression* represents a movement back into experience, from which
the novel can isolate itself only at the cost of total suicide. By
the 1950s, the conventions of the dominant realistic form in
this country had become a formula and realistic fiction had
lapsed into a dull formalism that began to incite widespread
claustrophobia among its audience, which consequently began to desert it. The success of the "new journalism" in the
sixties was a corollary of the novel's need to blast itself open
to experience again.

III. The Hermetic Digression

Consider William H. Gass's clever way around the concept
of imitation:

> Think, for instance, of a striding statue; imagine the purposeful in-
> clination of the torso, the alert and penetrating gaze of the head and
> its eyes, the outstretched arm and pointing finger; everything
> would appear to direct us toward some goal in front of it. Yet our
> eye travels only to the finger's end, and not beyond. Though point-
> ing, the finger bids us stay instead, and we journey slowly back
> along the tension of the arm. In our hearts we know what actually
> surrounds the statue. The same surrounds every other work of art:
> empty space and silence.[2]

In other words, fiction does not refer to a reality beyond itself. Okay. But given that art is not mimetic, it does not follow that it is hermetic. When we say that creative language is
nonreferential I take it we mean that it doesn't refer to other
language, other concepts—it points toward the mute world
beyond language, beyond history, and then itself falls silent.
Art is an escape from language and abstraction—and verbal
art is the most conclusive escape into our birthright in the
world beyond language from which language above all sepa-
rates us, and which, therefore, it has the power to restore. A
statue out of Wallace Stevens might serve as a commentary
on Gass's brilliant construction. Gass:

> But the writer must not let the reader out; the sculptor must not let
> the eye fall from the end of his statue's finger; the musician must
> not let the listener dream. Of course, he will; but let the blame be
> on himself. High tricks are possible; to run the eye rapidly along
> that outstretched arm to the fingertip, only to draw it up before it
> falls away in space; to carry the reader to the very edge of every
> word so that it seems he must be compelled to react as though to

truth as told in life, and then to return him like a philosopher liberated from the cave, to the clear and brilliant world of concept, to the realm of order, proportion, and dazzling construction.[3]

Stevens:

One feels the passion of rhetoric begin to stir and even to grow furious; and one thinks that, after all, the noble style, in whatever it creates, merely perpetuates the noble style. In this statue, the apposition between the imagination and reality is too favorable to the imagination.[4]

The good of rhetoric is to connect us with the world, not separate us from it. Art delivers us from abstraction and solipsism with a newly vitalized (lively) sense of experience. It does not cage us in the crystal perfection of art. When writing gets locked in the imagination it falls under the dominion of the "bawdo of euphony." Rhetoric. Literature This may account for the loneliness of Willie Master's wife. But while hermeticism devitalizes the work, it at least focuses attention on the validity of the artifact itself, from which *The Hermeneutic Digression* tends to distract us.

IV. The Hermeneutic Digression

There is an underlying dilemma of interpretation that theorists seem to feel the need to confront, as here Michel Foucault: "Commentary's only role is to say finally, what has silently been articulated deep down. It must—and the paradox is ever-changing yet inescapable—say, for the first time, what has already been said, and repeat tirelessly what was, nevertheless, never said."[5] I suppose one way out would be for criticism itself to become, as Harold Bloom suggests, a kind of prose poetry—a kind of second-rate fiction almost inevitably. It may be that the rushing wing of poetry will one day be joined by the wagging tail of thought, but it would seem more likely that poetry and fiction could incorporate theory (Valery, Joyce, Stevens) than the other way around. Perhaps one of the best things that can be said for theory is that it's a good way to get rid of theory. When a discipline becomes so detached that it becomes detached from its object, or even begins to displace it, you can be sure you are in for a certain amount of grotesquerie. A journalist thinks that journalism is not reportage but a kind of fiction, and a superior kind no less. Fine. Now where do I go to get the news? A literary critic evolves the position that essay is the essential art—and someone remarks that if he were a garbage collector he would think garbage collecting the central art. And why not? Today everything is art. The minimalists, "happenings" people, and pop artists have implied that life itself is art. The conceptualists tell us that ideas are art. Historians are begining to tell us that history is art. And now professors claim that scholarship is art. But surely Harold Bloom's thesis of interpretation as misinterpretation and criticism as poetry is an elaborate joke. What Bloom is trying to tell us is that it's time for interpretation to do away with itself, thereby completing the cycle of a Digression and releasing us once more, much enriched no doubt, into the experience of the poem. In *The Anxiety of Influence*, he speaks of "the mind's effort to overcome the impasse of Formalist criticism, the barren moralizing that Archetypal criticism has come to be, and the anti-humanistic plain dreariness of all those developments in European criticism that have yet to demonstrate that they can aid in reading any one poem by any poet whatsoever."[6] The subversive absurdity of Bloom's thesis can only be a Pataphysical stratagem to return us from poetics to poetry and fiction.

V. The Conceptual Digression

The tenacity of fiction as imitation in our culture is not due merely to the sloth or ignorance of the publishing establishment, or even to its greed. We are a schizoid culture and have an enormous investment in our own neurosis. The idea of art as a mirror sustains a disconnected, emotionally dissociated attitude toward experience. Such art presents us with an image of our experience in a way that assures us it is not real: it is a reflection, only a picture, only a story—at last, a way of defining our experience in a form in which we do not have to take responsibility for it. The mode that must have been a means of meditation for Vermeer becomes for us, as cliché, a form of limited liability, a way of packaging our experience so that we can walk away from it. What we call realism saps our experience of its immediacy and authority, a process tremendously augmented by the electronic media and probably one reason for their great success. It is as if your fundamental image of yourself and your life were the one on the television screen, as if we were all actors playing roles. Those "primitives" who are said to feel that snapshots can steal your soul are correct. Finally it is the image on the screen that has all the reality, and experience becomes "fact" only, as they say, when you see it on the evening news. In the sixties we developed two ways of getting rid of the mirror of art. One is that the mirror is an illusion, it doesn't exist, there's no difference between art and life: *The Experiential Digression*. The second is that the art work exists only in the realm of the mind and therefore is not a mirror but a window which requires no embodiment: *The Conceptual Digression*. Both are assaults on the idea of art as artifact. The degree of excess that developed in these two Digressions is an index to the urgency behind them. Art as a window implies that it is a means to reach some end other than itself. What? Can we seriously entertain ideas of transcendence? Those faery lands forlorn seen through the magic casement are forlorn precisely because they don't exist. If they did, perhaps a concept would be sufficient as a means of transporting us to them and the work of art as a sensuous artifact might be redundant. Possibly that ephemeralization so dear to the Post-Catholic Post-Moderns like McLuhan, Soleri, and William Irwin Thompson might then seem more appropriate. Conceptual art dematerializes the art work and moves us toward mounting levels of abstraction. At the same time it moves us away from that union of sense and concept, matter and spirit, ego and world toward which our desire for wholeness of experience impels us and that occurs in a successfully embodied work of art. For that reason, ideas cheapen fiction when they dominate its form, as they do for example in those popular science fiction–fantasy paintings by Escher, and that may be the trouble with so-called "speculative fiction," now being advanced by some eminent critics as the new wave. On the other hand, as an analytic reflex, conceptual art is extremely useful for fiction. It destroys the idea of the novel as a consumer item and teaches us that fiction is an event in the field of experience that, like many other events, has the power to alter that field in significant ways. Conceptual art may also be a way of reclaiming the discursive for a tradition that has proceeded largely in terms of connotation throughout the modern period. Furthermore, *The Conceptual Digression* in effect constitutes an attempt to confront and work through one side of our schizophrenic split between thought and experience. *The Experiential Digression* is an attempt to work through the other side.

VI. The Experiential Digression

This involves the question of the frame. If art is continuous with experience, there is no frame. Art is free, at last, actually to merge with life. Artists in the sixties were finding all sorts of ways of moving out of the frame. On one side happenings, on the other Segal's plaster casting of reality. Frank O'Hara, in a half-serious statement reprinted in a "New York School" anthology which the editors claim "in many ways speaks for us all," talks about writing a poem for a lover:

While I was writing it I was realizing that if I wanted to I could use the telephone instead of writing the poem, and so Personism was born. It's a very exciting movement which will undoubtedly have lots of adherents. It puts the poem squarely between the poet and the person, Lucky Pierre style, and the poem is correspondingly gratified. The poem is at last between two persons instead of two pages. In all modesty, I confess that it may be the death of literature as we know it.[7]

The thrust of O'Hara's poetry, which was to claim the continuity of poetry with experience as against its discontinuity in terms of technique, abstraction, or content, was an enormous contribution. And I agree that art must continually kill itself—but it always has to make sure it's art that does the killing. The obvious step for the literal minded, after O'Hara's

statement, is that the poem is unnecessary. Aha! Art is life—
just as we thought, so who needs art? This leaves one open to
The Experiential Digression, the latest form of the ongoing
American conspiracy against art in favor of "real life," also
known as "fact." Unless a line is drawn, the horde of Factists
blunder in waving their banner on which it is written: "It
really happened." Here is Tom Wolfe defending the new
journalism against fiction: "The reader knows *all this actually
happened* [italics his]. The disclaimers have been erased. The
screen is gone. The writer is one step closer to the absolute involvement of the reader that Henry James and James Joyce
dreamed of and never achieved."[8] This is what James and
Joyce dreamed of? Too bad they didn't work for the Hearst
chain. This is the harvest of the doctrine of willing suspension
of disbelief: if art is illusion, then documentary is better because it's the real thing. But on another level, the question of
the frame has been a troublesome one ever since action painting made a point of the continuity of the act of composition
with the rest of experience. The idea that fiction has no special essence releases a lot of energy, but if it hasn't then why
not journalism? Why not journals? Why not graphics? Why
not comic books? Why not anything? With the loss of the
frame, notes critic Richard Pearce, the medium of fiction
"asserts itself as an independent and vital part of the subject," and citing Beckett as an example goes on to say that the
medium "comes to dominate the narrator, the characters,
and the story."[9] That is perhaps the most significant difference between fiction in the sixties and fiction in the seventies.
The latter has dropped the sixties' sense of irony about the
form, its guilty conscience about the validity of the novel, its
self-parody and self-consciousness. That self-consciousness
has become, in the seventies, a more acute consciousness
about the medium and its options.

VII. The Concrete Digression

Of writers working innovatively with the medium of fiction, among the most visible are those who are most visually oriented. Concrete Poetry or, as I call it, Cement Poetry, with its heavy-handed sense of writing as a visual artifact, confounds issues by mistaking what the medium is. The discursive aspect of language can be ignored only at the risk of crossing the line between literature and graphics, and if it comes to that, I would rather look at Picasso. With the seventies' new consciousness of fiction as a medium, however, it becomes apparent that part of the medium is the look of print on the page. Page arrangement has become a factor in composition that many writers are working with, including Steve Katz, Peter Matthiessen, George Chambers, and Raymond Federman. Such writers have transformed the visual element of fiction from an implicit and inert compositional factor to an expressive one. The masterpiece of this current in seventies fiction is Federman's recent *Take It Or Leave It*,[10] which retains the communicative aspect of language by using it as a kind of melody played against the rhythm of radical page arrangement. It is the most successful attempt I know of to recognize and resolve the tension between the communicative and visual aspects of fiction.

VIII. The Oral Digression

The Oral Digression is complementary to *The Concrete Digression*, and proposes the spoken aspect of language as the essential literary element. The Oral Digression has had more influence on poetry than fiction, partly due to the inevitable preponderance of poetry on the reading circuit. The idea is abroad—propagated by such figures as Ginsberg, Snider, and some of the third-world writers—that the ultimate context of poetry is the reading. Its influence has also been felt by fiction writers, and we are beginning to see such interesting mistakes as *Black Box*, the tape-recorded magazine. The influence has been in some respects beneficial. Written language draws much vitality from spoken language, and the further it moves from the voice the greater the risk that it will go dead. That is why composition by tape recorder can be suggestive and energizing. But composition and finished artifact are two different things. Fiction, finally, involves print on a page, and that is not an incidental convenience of production and distribution, but an essential of the medium.

IX. The Collagist Digression

It is now a commonplace that collage has been central to the modern and postmodern movements. Once the frame has been broken, there is no a priori form and works have to be patched together, or, at least, that is one way to go about it. Thus Donald Barthelme's much quoted comment that he only trusts fragments. The idea of collage has, in fact, become a cliché, and like all clichés, is misleading. While the broken frame leads to fragmentation, it is a fertile fragmentation that precedes the invention of new, if impermanent, form. To speak of fragments is to imply that finished and successful works remain fragmented, and this is not the case. We think in fragments and we compose in fragments, but the fictive art consists precisely in the use of the medium to compose out of fragments viable wholes. The medium in question is neither language in general, nor speech, but writing, which has it own reality and particular power. "Imagining," writes

Jean Ricardou, "and *imagining pen in hand* [italics his] are two entirely distinct activities. . . . Exercising the imagination while at the same time apprehending its movement—such is the privilege that writing seems to enjoy. The written fragment is not flight, mobility, disappearance, but rather inscription, a stable reference. With it, imagination changes status."[11] Composition, in other words, is no longer controlled by the demands of the frame, nor is it left as a dynamic collocation of fragments whose form is indeterminate, but proceeds in and through the text to the creation of formal wholes which may be strange, surprising, and should be unpredictable, even to the author. Such fiction is akin to what George Chambers, in his novel *The Bonnyclabber*, calls "going-ungoing" which involves a deferral of intention: "The word means that one is and is not going where one is going. It allows one to feel surprise and thus pleasure, even amidst the ordinary operations of the everyday day. . . . Every step an adventure."[12] This kind of fiction is not "about" anything except itself, that is, about the way we structure event through language, which is to say, finally, that it is about almost everything.

X. The Experimental Digression

I don't write experimental fiction. None of the writers I have mentioned in these remarks writes experimental fiction. If you want to know about experimental fiction, get in touch with Richard Kostelanetz. All good fiction today, in whatever form, is exploratory with regard to the medium and highly conscious of it—even realistic narrative, given the context of the seventies that it must take into account. Therefore Experimental Fiction is no longer a valid category, if it ever was. Aren't we really tired of the stale categories on the basis of which we mechanically conduct the same boring discourse about the future of the novel? Experimental versus conventional, new novel versus old novel, linear versus nonlinear, commercial versus noncommercial, realism, surrealism, avant-gardism, modernism, postmodernism, the whole batch needs to be thrown overboard. Fiction writers today are writing from a point of view well anterior to the genres and subgenres of the novel. They begin by questioning the medium itself, and their work involves an exploration of the idea of fiction, not only in the novel, but in the culture at large. There is no such thing as fiction. Instead there is a continuing fictive discourse which continually redefines itself. There is certainly no such thing as THE novel. Instead there are as many novels as there are authentic novelists, and, ideally, there should be as many novels as there are novels of those novelists, since in an exploratory situation, every form should be idiosyncratic. Fiction itself proceeds by digression and cannot be predicted or defined. Each novel is a unique definition, a definition of itself. It follows that our criticism of fiction should make a progressive effort to defamiliarize the novel, to de-define fiction, as fiction simultaneously creates and decreates itself.

1977

Eight Digressions on the Politics of Language

I

Literary values serve the interests of classes, groups, professions, institutions, industries, and this is neither bad nor avoidable. But it is a factor consistently omitted from discussion of contemporary literature—and that omission in itself, no doubt, is in somebody's interest. From this point of view, literary judgment can be read as a code, a code it might be in the interest of some literary people to maintain, and of others to break. In any case, such factors as circumstances of publication, the publishing situation, the condition of the market, the structure of production and distribution, socioeconomic and political considerations, are legitimate areas of study bearing on literary composition, style, criticism, literary history, and evaluation. Not long ago I had an argument with Susan Sontag, the important critic-novelist-filmmaker. It began when Sontag said that all American writers are one another's enemies. The group of French professors to whom she was speaking immediately asked: what about the Fiction Collective? Sontag then replied that the Fiction Collective was based solely on the principle of exclusion, meaning, I presume, that those excluded by the publishing industry could have nothing in common other than their various miscellaneous reasons for having been excluded. I responded that, on the contrary, working outside the industry provided these novelists with the opportunity to develop styles that one could develop only with difficulty, if at all, were one being published by the industry and subject to its commercial pressures. I said that such an alternative allowed new voices to be heard and new criteria to develop. Sontag replied that there were no such things as new criteria, that the relevant criteria were the same for ourselves as they had been for Shakespeare. I took this to be the wisdom of the establishment. When one is at the center of the literary establishment, as Sontag is, it is not in one's interest to notice competing claims. The question here is not whether there are in fact new voices worth hearing outside the publishing industry, but whether there are extraliterary considerations that modify literary standards. The resistance one encounters to this possibility is interesting. The attitude that one's own criteria are the only possible criteria is a denial of the interplay of social, economic, and literary forces that are part of the larger context of a work. Denying the politics of language (as opposed to literary politics, which is a different matter) is only another way of using them.

II

The politics of language is a phrase that seems justified in connection with literary values because discussion of the way such values are formed and what they imply leads to ques-

tions about control of the language. Such issues usually surface in times of conflict. The battle between academic and
Beat poets at the beginning of the sixties was the consequence
of certain political, economic, and demographic changes.
But it was not only a consequence, it was also part of the
broader social struggle. I remember an exchange that took
place at the time involving Gregory Corso, who, in response
to a heckler, said: "Why are you making fun of the way I
talk? I'm not making fun of the way you talk." Of course the
Beats were in one way or another constantly making fun of
the prevailing literary establishment. They gave the impression of having a lot more fun with the establishment than the
establishment was having by itself, and finally, by appearing
more attractive, by identifying with a youthful audience, and
by compelling more attention, they forced the establishment
to react to them seriously, to play their game. The literary
war was fought on nonliterary grounds. The result was that
one way of talking and of writing gained enormously in prestige, and another lost. A new vocabularly, new rhythms, new
forms, and new models in writing helped prepare and support the liberation movements of the sixties. About a year
ago I saw Corso introducing Allen Ginsberg—who now runs
a creative writing program—and Corso was wearing a suit
and tie. Ginsberg then performed a long poem that sounded
to me a lot like a Dryden masque (though Ginsberg told me
the diction was out of Blake). Corso's tie is an item in literary
history, a subject for scholarly speculation. The politics of
language have changed. Presidential candidates write poetry.
Governor Jerry Brown is a friend of Gary Snyder. Everyone
can write a poem like William Carlos Williams, and almost
everyone does. The whole middle class has joined the underground. The government supports the literary magazines.
The sixties rhetoric of rebellion has joined with the main-

stream, and we are left without a potent language of dissent. In much contemporary fiction and poetry, a manner not very different from the language pasteurized and homogenized by the media prevails: U.S. Standard English. Language and form are becoming more standardized and are supported by federal, state, and city tax money, as well as by commerical profit. The politics of that situation seem clear.

III

One line of scholarly research in contemporary letters might be the connections between the Mafia and mass paperback distribution. What effect does that have on current literary theory? Because it has one. It helps to determine what books can be sold, and that in turn affects the circumstances of composition within which one thinks about the nature, the form, and the purpose of one's work. I don't mean that one allows salability to condition style, as in the best-seller business, though it is refreshing to remember that such models of the underground as Joyce, Henry Miller, Beckett, and Raymond Roussel all harbored ideas of popularity. Once in an article for *Partisan Review* I suggested the possibility of a new popular audience for innovative fiction, and William Phillips told me that was a contradiction in terms, a familiar illusion for American writers. No doubt, but the attempt to resolve such contradictions can provide useful tensions in one's work. One thinks of a theoretical audience that helps in breaking out of the hermeticism of the modern tradition, not, unfortunately, cash customers. The publishing situation conditions that sort of speculation, as well as the rhetoric one employs. I don't want to blame publishing on the Mafia, but the steady closing of the market to quality books during the last ten years due to factors such as corporate conglomeration and increasing monopolization of the means of distribution has had an interesting and not altogether negative effect on the rhetoric of fiction. The shortest way to put it is that the audience for poetry and the audience for quality fiction is becoming the same audience, and that many fiction writers now share the premises, models, and expectations of that audience. One certainly cannot discuss the theory of American fiction of the last fifteen years without establishing its continuities with the poetics of the last sixty. Few serious writers will now draw a line between poetry and fiction, and many poets are themselves turning to the novel. Perhaps because American poetry has already had its revolution while fiction is still going through the throes, and perhaps partly also because the novel is still a form that has great potential market value (I once infuriated a Hollywood novelist simply by mentioning one of my titles, *The Death of the Novel*), the urgent poetic concerns tend to come up these days in the context of fiction. You can do anything you want in a poem and nobody will get irritated, but I notice that books like *Naked Lunch* can still send students into an angry frenzy, and that was published twenty years ago. The forms of fiction, apparently, are still felt as relevant to the facts of life, and that, politically speaking, implies a certain amount of power.

IV

Why do many people in the publishing industry tend to take a moral tone toward nonconventional fiction? It is almost as if writing a nonmimetic novel were an act of social irresponsibility. My agent has received rejection notices from editors who are not content with merely turning my work down but feel impelled to write long diatribes on the nature of my fiction—and I am not talking about hack commercial editors, but the ones with reputations as friends of literature. A clue may be found in a recent attack on the Fiction Collective by a reviewer who takes the standard line of the industry since it closed down to nonconventional writing at the end of the sixties: "Anything traditional or too easily understood makes an academic fiction writer vulnerable to charges that he is a literal-minded simpleton or a shameless panderer to mass tastes. Once upon a time, part of fiction's appeal was in bringing to a broad middle-class audience parts of the world—geographical, sociological, or what have you—remote from that audience's ordinary experience." First of all, there is the implication here that difficulty and complexity are a betrayal of the democratic mandate. There are literary criteria, supposedly academic, that are contemptuous of the masses—though no distinction is made between the masses and the mass market, which are two very different things. "Mass tastes," evidently, have nothing to do with the proletariat but rather with "a broad middle-class audience." Fiction used to appeal to that audience "once upon a time," but it seems there is some question whether it still does so. In any case, it should. Any alternate criteria are going to further threaten the coherence of the mass market for fiction. What that market needs, apparently, is fiction that is remote from its "ordinary experience." Why? Dickens was a muckraker. Dreiser and Hemingway wrote pointedly about our everyday experience and, in fact, that is the main thrust of the great American realistic tradition in fiction. But the mass market is not only an economic entity, it is also necessarily a political entity the manipulation of whose imagination renders it politically manageable as well as financially profitable. Thus the last thing wanted is to increase the consumer's awareness of his own experience. This has stylistic consequences: what is required is a language and form that is standardized so that it can be merchandised to the largest number of people, that is hypnotic and diverting, drawing attention away from ordinary experience and into an anesthetic formula that is familiar and reassuring. Plot, character, verisimilitude, and U.S. Standard English, vendable to film companies and paperback houses which is where the big audience is, and the big money. In the controversy between conventional and nonconventional fiction, market values are disguised as literary values. In fact, for the publishing industry literary values are beside the point when you come down to it. A remark made by a *New York Times* daily book reviewer is symptomatic: in praising E. L. Doctorow's *Ragtime*, he called it an experimental novel that everyone can understand.

V

If money is a kind of poetry, as Wallace Stevens observed, then language can be regarded as a kind of currency or, as Robert Frost said, everything comes to market. It is only when the terms of the market are disguised that this becomes destructive. There seems to be an ephemeral metalanguage in the publishing industry, used to resolve contradictions between publishing as business enterprise and publishing as cultural institution, of which someone should do a glossary, if only for the sake of those young writers who take it to express purely literary values. "Experimental novel," for example, means something like "no sales of subsidiary rights." "Run it through the typewriter again" means "we don't know if we want to publish it, but we'd like to keep you on the hook so that no one else does while we make up our minds." "It will just go down the tubes" means "I like the manuscript but nobody here including me thinks it will make any money so they won't push it so it won't make any money." And so on. There is nothing wrong with making money, but there seems to be a scale of bluntness about it in the industry, with editorial people on the lower end. A Dell salesman once told me, "I haven't read your book and I probably won't, but my wife tried it and wanted me to ask you one question." "What's that?" I said. "Are you kidding?" he responded. At a sales party I had a long conversation with a woman I assumed to be a salesperson in which I explained why one of my books wasn't picked up as a "quality" paperback, not because it lacked quality but because it wasn't sufficiently commercial. She agreed enthusiastically and even elaborated on my argument. We understood one another perfectly. She turned out to be Helen Meyer, at that time owner of Dial, Delta, and Dell.

Editorial doubletalk, on the other hand, leads to doublethink. At a symposium of writers and editors on the problem of publishing quality fiction, the writers were repeatedly told by the editors that they would like to publish more quality fiction, but the market being what it is for such books, they couldn't afford to do so. When alternative means of publishing such fiction were then suggested, however, the editorial response was, "Don't worry, if anything worth publishing comes along we'll publish it." As Jonathan Baumbach, one of the key founders of the Fiction Collective states the situation: "Really good books will have large audiences, they tell us, pointing to Dickens and the latest middlebrow best-seller, and besides no one is buying serious fiction. The delusions necessary to keep a clear conscience make an ideology out of an unadmitted cynicism." Reviewers and writers supported by the industry tend to pick up the party line. In politics, people take a position based on the necessities of power, regardless of contradictions, fact, or ethics, then turn to the propagandists and say, "We need some language for this"—that is, plausible formulas that can be repeated again and again to answer critics. This, then, is the "language" of the publishing industry. And so a structure of evaluation proliferates based on an initial mystification that by weight of repetition and sheer domination of the means of production and communication set standards of taste. Even those academics interested in contemporary writing are often carried along, not so much by the "language" involved as by an exaggerated American respect for the wisdom of the "real world" (i.e., business world) as opposed to the value of intellectual discipline. The degree to which academics and "intellectuals" can be flattered and intimidated by that world is surprising. Thus those who one might expect to be the last line of defense against this sort of thing sometimes seem to lack ideological conviction or even, at times, self-respect. I attended a symposium on contemporary fiction organized by an important academic journal devoted to the subject, and which was conducted at a reasonable level of scholarship and theoretical concern. At a certain point a commerical novelist whom I had never heard of, but who happened to be teaching at the university involved, was given a short time to address the assembled scholars. What he said, in effect, was that he was a real novelist, that the deliberations of the symposium made no sense to him, and that he thought the whole business was completely worthless. The response of the participants was enthusiastic and extended applause.

VI

Why is it so often said that in America writers are one another's enemies? Because, I think, it is generally true. Until such time as factories—that is, computer centers—can take over the production of the schlock, nonbooks, and formula fiction that publishers manufacture, writing will remain a cottage industry, a craft practiced at home in isolation, a matter of piecework. The writer's professional relations are not fraternal but filial. The editor is father and the agent mother. When a group of novelists, including me, got together in 1974 to talk about starting its own publishing conduit as a way of resisting the publishing industry, we gradually began to realize that we were getting involved in something more complicated than simply providing an alternate means of publication. There was a strong psychological barrier that kept us from moving ahead. Without at all realizing it, we were making a transition from a paternal to a fraternal mode, a transition that met with powerful emotional resistance, but that released a great deal of energy when it was finally made. For example, all of the founding writers had published, and most had dealt extensively with commercial houses, had several books out, and were writers of established reputation. Despite the fact that we felt most editors had the literary discrimination of used-car salesmen, and knew that even good editors had to make decisions heavily conditioned by commercial considerations, we soon realized that emotionally our sanction as writers still came from the publishers. We had our opinions of our own and of our contemporaries' work, but a big contract from Random House somehow canceled our literary criteria. Further, acceptance by a publishing house still represented acceptance as a real writer. In competing for this approval, as well as for advances, publicity, and the backing of editors and agents, we were in fact one another's enemies. We were working for the boss. The boss had the power to enable us to earn a living or not, to make or break our careers, to decide whether our work was good or worthless. This was completely at odds with our image of the writer as the most independent spirit in the culture, creating new ways and new standards. Actually, we were just playing the game, providing the boss with a product to sell if and when he thought it would be worth money to him.

Writing, unlike industrial labor in which you are guaranteed pay as long as you have work, is craft labor, in which you first produce the product, then try to sell it. The craftsman is always in a vulnerable, often powerless situation. When the Fiction Collective decided, in its own small way, to "seize the means of production and distribution," it was an assertion of power, a symbolic act of rebellion, a move toward realization of the ideal of writer as free spirit, demiurge, critic of the zeitgeist. It also represented a psychological liberation in a culture that tends to infantilize its artists: you must be helpless, irresponsible, and self-destructive—or else. Or else what? Or else you're not a real artist. But there is one other factor. Publishers are not just ordinary bosses; they are word bosses. They have enormous power to decide what language is good and what language is bad, and to back up those decisions by saturating the market with millions of copies of their books. Language control is mind control. At one time not so long ago, publishing was a somewhat genteel business, and many houses were family owned or bore the imprint of a particular personality and had some kind of independent taste, even if bad. But to have our language largely under the control of a handful of conglomerates like Gulf and Western, which along with a few other octopi control almost everything else, is a new situation. It is extremely odd that the Fiction Collective, with its tiny list of six books a year in face of the thousands and thousands pumped out by the industry, should have caused such a fuss, that it still, after five years, annoys the publishers and arouses controversy. It must be at least partly because if you think about the Collective at all, you have to think about these issues.

VII

It is estimated that there are now fifteen hundred little magazines in America, and of these at least seven hundred are purely literary magazines. The number increases every year. They and the presses associated with them represent a fascinating variety of opinions, literary attitudes, regional and ethnic perspectives. They range from mimeo sheets to professional productions rivaling the slicks, and cost from less than fifty to far more than five thousand dollars per issue. They publish many of the worst writers in the country and many of the best, some of whom never publish with the slicks or the big publishers. It is a world of its own that has very little to do with the publishing industry which, in fact, pays very little attention to it. Nevertheless, most well-known writers started their publishing careers in it, and many continue to publish in it after they have been published by the big presses. It is a major American literary and social phenomenon which merits much more scholarly study than it has so far received. Though the audience for the small presses and magazines is small—some have more contributors than subscribers—they continue to proliferate. None make money. Many cease publication after a few issues. The impulse behind them, I think, is an impulse toward freedom, an expression of particularity, an assertion of individual power. While the big publishers seek the mass market with increasingly standardized products, the small ones accomodate the quirky and isolated artist—that most of the editors are also writers goes without saying—and in so doing start, if not a mass movement, at least a "grass-roots" one. But how much of what the small presses and magazines turn out is good writing?

For some years I was associated with, and for two years I was Chairman of the Board of, the Coordinating Council of Literary Magazines, an organization to which almost all the literary magazines belong and which helps support them through grants, promotion, advocacy, and general services. It is completely controlled by writers and literary magazine editors. At the time I was Chairman it had a budget of about a million a year from the National Endowment for the Arts, the New York State Council on the Arts, the Ford Foundation, and other sources. The main function of the organization was to give grants to the magazines on the basis of "quality and need." Need was easy to determine. The problem was, how do you define quality? We felt that there were too many magazines. We felt that there were too many bad magazines. We saw that our grants were encouraging a multiplication of mediocrity that threatened to bury the best work being done. But we had a Board that was chosen to represent the most inclusive possible spectrum of literary taste by region, kind of magazine, ethnic grouping, and so on. In discussions about how to define quality, the very term became suspect. Every group saw that a particular definition of quality could be used against it. At one point Ishmael Reed, who was on the Board, said that quality was just a code word for "white." We were confronted in a very practical way with the question of literary criteria, and we kept discovering that literary criteria often break down, when challenged, into the social, regional, economic, ethnic, and ideological considerations from which they were derived. I became keenly aware that my own literary standards were not "pure," but represented the things in which I had a stake, as in fact they should. And yet in all this it turned out that a substantial part of the criteria could be based on formal values inherent in a certain amount of common tradition and the way we use American English. The grants were awarded by committees whose majority was elected by the magazine community. It was surprising to see the extent to which writers and editors from completely different corners of the small press world could agree on what was good writing and what was bad. There were many areas of dispute. They were settled by persuasion, argument, compromise, and finally by vote.

And how, in fact, are disputed areas of taste handled in the larger literary world? Will invoking Shakespeare do the trick? Do we have an authority to which we can appeal to settle such questions? Do we want one? It is true there were stupidities perpetrated by those committees: for example, the committee that decided to divide the amount of money available by the number of applicants and award each magazine the same amount, whether they had budgets of fifty or five thousand dollars, thus giving some magazines enough to buy their scratch pads, and others much more than they knew what to do with. But then, that was an outspokenly populist committee with an explicit prejudice in favor of the smaller, cheaper, less sophisticated magazines. It seems to me that if public discourse about what constitutes good writing were carried on with the same bluntness and openness it might be an improvement, and might keep evaluation more honest, critical language more straightforward, and literary standards more rooted in the realities of our lives. And how good is the writing in the small presses compared to that in the big ones? By my own standards, I would say the level of mediocrity is more various, more lively, less stifling, and that this is directly traceable to the degree of control the writers have over their artistic lives in the small press scene.

VIII

The Fiction Collective and the Coordinating Council of Literary Magazines are unique efforts in this country to give writers a measure of control over their artistic fate as against the practical monopoly of commercial mass production and distribution (there are other, more successful, examples in European countries). Production and distribution must develop together, since there is little point in producing books and magazines that cannot find their appropriate audience. The Fiction Collective has used a sympathetic commercial publisher, George Braziller, as its distributor. CCLM was awarded a Ford Foundation grant of about a half million dollars to start to set up a distribution system for small magazines and presses, though we found that this was just enough to intiate cooperative distribution efforts by the magazine community. Finally one runs up against two problems which are in fact inseparable. The first is the very limited number of bookstores that are willing to handle literary publications not distributed by the publishing industry, and the absence of any mail-order or book-club arrangement that might bypass the bookstores. The second and more interesting problem is the lack of an adequate flow of information about writing produced outside of the publishing industry.

Concerning the first problem, there is probably no answer other than an influx of capital from the government or the foundations to support a distribution network substantial enough to give it a chance to become self-sustaining, though it should be noted that we do not expect our opera and ballet companies, our museums, our symphony orchestras, our repertory companies, or our library system to support themselves. Sooner or later we are going to have to recognize that serious contemporary literature is becoming more and more a nonprofit industry. Already large numbers of our serious writers are being supported by university creative writing programs. Perhaps it is time that college bookstores replace some of their teddy bears and beer mugs with literary magazines and small press books, and for university presses regularly to include quality fiction and poetry in their lists. Perhaps it is time also for the National Endowment for the Humanities to recognize the educational function of serious contemporary writing. Admittedly, university, government, and foundation support has its dangers for creative freedom, but so do increasingly oppressive commerical pressures. The best safeguard would seem to be balancing one source of support against another.

As to the second problem, means have not existed to inform the public adequately, or even the writing community itself, about what is being done in contemporary writing. First of all, the literary scene is fractured into many worlds that share a common ignorance about one another. The split between the publishing industry and the small presses is only the most obvious of these. The world of the small presses is itself byzantine in its rivalries and insular in its myriad groupings. And while review coverage for the important literary work from the large presses has been inadequate, for the small presses it has been nonexistent. To a surprising extent American writing as a whole is still an unknown quantity, even to its practitioners, not to mention editors, critics, and scholars. The real litcrary situation in this country has not crystallized yet for lack of information. When it does it may prove to be more complex and more distinctively American than most people suspect. For one thing, we need to confront the prospect, which some writers are beginning to talk about, of a transition to a "post-European" culture, for better or for worse. This position involves the belief that we must come to terms with a uniquely American situation. The Anglomania of the *New York Review of Books* may be the last stand of a tradition increasingly difficult to sustain. At the very least, America is no longer an "Anglo-Saxon" culture, as the French so insultingly insist on calling it. The emergence of various ethnic sensibilities—Black, Hispanic, Jewish, Oriental, and Native American, among others—is eroding the dominance of U.S. Standard English and its attendant forms of expression which, it seems, can no longer even be taught very effectively in the schools. It perhaps no longer makes any sense to talk about "experimental" fiction or "avant-garde" poetry. What we may be seeing is a complicated shift in literary forms reflecting a major shift in cultural sensibility that is partly ethnic, and still more the result of swift technological advance and social disruption. If this is true, it would be a shift in taste very different from the kind that took place during the elitist, hermetic, and politically reactionary modern movement, though it might be deeply rooted in it. In any case it seems to me that our criticism will lack authority and our literature remain tentative until we have a more complete sense of what is happening in contemporary American writing. A number of writers, recognizing the need for a better source of information about American writing, have participated in the founding of the *American Book Review*, now in its second year of publication, which covers writing from the large, small, regional, third-world, and university presses, including especially work—books of poetry, first novels, unconventional writing—poorly covered by the established reviewing media. Our main audience is other writers, and by providing this crucial group with an overview of American writing we hope to crystallize emerging shifts in taste or criteria. We hope it will also be the modest beginning of a needed effort to widen the scope of critical attention in contemporary American letters. Finally, the creation of an adequate medium of contemporary literary information is an important link in the chain of writer-controlled institutions—means of publication, of funding, of distribution—necessary to sustain a free creative language in resistance to commercial values now so pervasive they are starting to be taken for granted and accepted by academics, intellectuals, and, most dangerously, by artists themselves.

1979

Nine Digressions on Narrative Authority

I. The Politics of Authority

When we talk about "reality" with regard to fiction, what we're really talking about is the authority to comment plausibly on experience. The concept of "realism" in fiction is notoriously literary; that is, it depends on a set of rules for composition, now conventional, and understood all too well by a reader even superficially educated in our literary tradition who can acquiesce to them without the least thought, as if he were reading a newspaper. But the novel at least, without considering other forms of fiction, is distinguished, "realistic" or not, by its claim on a consensual reality, and has even functioned as a major medium of transition between experience—with all its implications of personalism, subjectivity, and, at the limit, solipsism—and "reality" which, "as everybody knows, is precisely that which everybody knows." A word must be said immediately for that subjectivity which the novel, from one point of view, is always striving to escape. It is just that subjectivity, that sense of individual experience, that is most threatened by media, propaganda, cliché and the "literary," by which I mean writing that depends too much on the accumulating "text" of the culture. Yes, culture, if not experience, can be considered as an ever-expanding text. Why not? But in fact life is not a book, not even cultural life, and any consideration of what gives prestige and authority to a text—appeals to tradition, "taste" and other mysteries of expertise notwithstanding—without accounting for questions of social class, economics, the politics of culture and pure accident is, to reinstitute a term popular in the sixties, phony. The establishment, of course, is always eager to profit from an illusion of "standards" based on the clichés of consumer manipulation and the static effect of tradition at the expense of individual experience. This is to say, simply, that literature is not the sanction for literature. Personally, I'm quite certain there is an argument to be made in justification of literature on a purely formal basis, but it probably would have more to do with neurology than literary tradition, which is too compromised by history to provide criteria not contingent on other areas of experience. So, from another point of view, we can consider the novel as an instrument that undercuts official versions of reality in favor of our individual sense of experience, now constantly threatened by the brain wash of politics and the mass market. Deviations from the latter in the direction of individual experience are labelled "narcissistic," "self-indulgent" and "pretentious." Marketing reduces tradition itself to slogans and nostalgia, compelling intellectuals to consider seriously such alternatives as "pop" and "camp." These are ploys which are illuminating insofar as they invert and therefore demystify "elitist" literary taste, but turning the dialogue upside down does not necessarily advance it. In any case, it's difficult to say which is more egregiously literary these days, the popular philosophy of the highbrow novel ne'er so well expressed, or the commercial imitators of a prior mode of realistic imitation whose practice is curiously in line with the recommendations of John Barth's view, before recent revision, that literature should imitate literature. This situation comes at the very moment, naturally, when no particular source of literary authority has any commanding intellectual sanction. The "literary establishment" is a notion that has become ambiguously literary as it becomes increasingly commercialized. Of the traditional alternatives, the avant-garde, in its ceaseless search for the new, has ceased to be importantly different, the "underground" was merchandised away by the sixties, and the "experimental" is a meaningless label. The literary elite, including the best critical minds, has moved to the university where practical criticism is often considered unworthy, a form of journalism, and many theorists are heavily involved in a new form of belles-lettres, encroaching on, rather than evaluating activity in the traditional genres. The matter of criteria in fiction has been left largely to the economics of the publishing industry which increasingly require formula commercial fiction, and the cultural sorties of the New Right, the only coherent group in view to grasp and exploit the connections among art, authority, and politics.

II. Realism

There is no contemporary Novel. The contemporary situation is rather that different kinds of novels may serve different purposes. The authority of the realistic/naturalistic mode is too deeply embedded in our tradition to lose its utility for fiction. There are persuasive reasons today for writing fiction in the realistic forms, even though such writing in no way repre-

sents "the state of the art." Realism, for example, can be useful during the emergence of a minority or oppressed culture
into increased consciousness. It can provide a means for the
presentation and evaluation of the data important to the life
of a cultural group when it most needs to hold the mirror up
to itself and its surrounding milieu. Naturalism may be especially useful to the phase when a subculture is beginning to
take stock of what it's all about and how it relates to other
parts of its world because of naturalism's cataloguing function; moreover, there is the fatalistic aspect of the naturalistic
novel which clarifies the relation of the individual to the necessities of industrial society. The *Studs Lonigan* series, though
stylistically an artifact from late nineteenth-century European fiction, was nevertheless appropriate to Irish-American
culture of the thirties. This kind of novel persuades because it
embodies the data of the culture as perceived by its members,
and the narrative point of view will go unchallenged because
it has the authority of their knowledge. But what happens to
such narrative authority when the data of a culture become
ambiguous? The status of the narrator must reflect the conditions of the historical moment or suffer a loss of credibility. In
Jane Bowles' *Two Serious Ladies*, for example, a novel that
evokes a certain cultural aimlessness and loss of certitude, we
have a narrative voice we can trust, but—or even because—
there is a kind of intentional feathering off into the unknown
and the ambiguous. This voice comprises a form of omniscient narration that, if not actually influenced by Kafka
(which is neither here nor there) must be looked at in view of
Kafka. That is, in Kafka we have omniscient narration, but
it's omniscient narration in which part of the omniscience is,
paradoxically, awareness of its limits. The normal situation
of the omniscient narrator is inverted. What the narrative
voice knows is the extent of the unknown. This may be om-

niscient narration technically, but intellectually, spiritually, it is the reverse of the Victorian voice of authority which implies that everything, if not known, is at least knowable. In Kafka, the narrative voice implies that you may think you know quite a bit but in fact you know very little and the more you look at things the less knowable they are until, finally, there is very little, if anything, you know at all. Realism, insofar as it is a component of Kafka's style, retains its authority only through its admission that reality is unknowable. The narrative situation there is not totally unlike the effect of the flood of information in a Pynchon novel, which by its very excess becomes finally ambiguous. If we admit the authority of Kafka's example, it conditions the use of the realistic form in a terminal way. There are, of course, levels in the culture where the rules may be clear and the essentials of the locale knowable—a regional or heavily class-defined setting, enclaves like the academic world, the homosexual world— and where the authority of the narrator's knowledge may go unquestioned. But one might risk the generalization that at present the authority of the realistic form is a self-conscious one, including an awareness of its limits as well as of its alternatives. *The French Lieutenant's Woman* would be a case in point. Another would be Rudolfo Anaya's *Bless Me Ultima*, whose incorporation of the magical from the Chicano tradition into the style of what might be called "anglo-realism," expands the limits of the latter in the direction of Latin American "Magic Realism."

III. Fragmentation

In *The Sound and the Fury* and *As I Lay Dying* the authority of realism is retained in a contingent way by establishing a narrative situation in which it appears that the truth may be arrived at through comparison of different, fragmented versions. This is, after all, one of our normal and accepted ways of arriving at truth, as in the testimony of witnesses in court, and is immediately persuasive at the level of common sense. It enters our literary tradition most obviously in the transition from, say, Edith Wharton to Henry James, or from early to late James. The persuasiveness of the contingent explains why a super-conscious writer like James would claim that a certain amount of stupidity is necessary in writing a good novel, a claim that complements the Jamesian strategy of reader obfuscation. The drive toward ambiguity in James and Conrad is not so far from Gide's techniques in *The Counterfeiters* to impede any tendency to assume a naïve version of reality, or even from Viktor Shklovsky's doctrine of "retardation," which has a similar effect. In Conrad a story is typically told through the incorporation—in the form itself—of the situation of limited narrative knowledge, implying that the reader not only cannot but should not trust a voice of total authority. Conrad's storytellers within the story constitute a reframing of the story from the point of view of contingency, because it is the contingent that is persuasive. In a book like Tom Glynn's novel, *Temporary Sanity*, the breakdown of narrative authority takes a peculiar democratic turn, in which the idea seems to be to investigate the populist mind and its limitations. The result is a book one of whose virtues is the description of how things seem from the point of view of stupidity, which creates another kind of contingent narrative authority. The narrative situation is similar in Michael Brownstein's persuasively lunatic *Country Cousins* and—but in terms of middle class blandness—in the fiction of James Schuyler. The area of authority for realism may have moved from description of social reality to description of points of view about it. Nabokov's eccentric narrative stances disclose not a common reality but the power of the imagination to affect it.

IV. The Reflexive

A quasi-religious mode that retains a certain amount of authority is that of testimony, or confession. If the novelist as god-the-father is no longer persuasive, a subjective or diaristic account of one's own experience would seem to be a rhetorically acceptable stance. That the mode crystallized by Henry Miller, however, now yields limited if attractive *tours de faiblesse* on the order of *Catcher in the Rye*, Frank Conroy's *Stop-time*, or, more recently, Jim Carroll's *The Basketball Diaries*, is no doubt indicative of our more sophisticated consciousness of the limits of language. Awareness of language as a coherent reality in itself, that both impedes and facilitates our description of experience, as—in the now familiar comparison—the instruments used in atomic physics interfere with the observation they make possible, quickly engenders a self-consciousness in the confessional mode, a consciousness, that is, of the effects of the instrument of observation. The consciousness that literature both reveals and falsifies experience is incorporated in the formal irony of fiction in the "death of the novel" or "literature of exhaustion" period at the end of the sixties. In the hands of a superconscious writer like Peter Handke, the confessional carries an awareness not only of the limits of that particular form of narration, but of the limits of language itself, so that the only way to retain the authority of the text is to incorporate that awareness of it. The narration then must turn back on itself. The reflexive texts of Genet and Beckett had already established textual self-reference as a condition of authenticity in the fifties. Their example has long since been taken into account by writers like Jonathan Baumbach, Walter Abish, Clarence Major and, in fact, almost every fiction writer working with the state of the art and, consequently, at the limits of the fictive imagination.

V. The Collective Voice

By the end of the sixties self-consciousness in terms of form became unavoidable, involving, as it did, the general sense of the limits of language and of the process of narration itself. One reaction to the personalism of the confessional mode, as well as to the apparent abstraction of the reflexive, was a move toward the authority of the collective voice. What I would call pseudo-mythology was a step toward such an alternative. This was an interest shared by such writers as Robert Coover, Steve Katz, John Barth, and William Gass, and was a trend parallel to that of the pseudo-autobiography utilized by some of the novelists writing in an apparently confessional mode that was in fact an imitation of that mode, like the "true histories" of the eighteenth century. A problem with myth, however, is that it's antihistorical, so that what is gained in authority by retelling traditional stories of one sort or another may be lost in the sense that they are "only stories." Once a myth is recognized as such, its fictive component is emphasized and its lack of innocence becomes obvious. Among the more fruitful influences in this area was that of the Latin American novelists in their use of a collective voice. I take it that the South Americans had antecedents in an important North American voice, Faulkner, who, however influenced by Joyce, is very different from him in that his collective voice is not that of "the tradition." In the Americas, where we work without a tradition comparable to that of Europe—where it might even be said that we have a basically antitraditional attitude—the resort to a collective voice will inevitably have a very distinctive character, neither mythic nor traditional, but a common voice credible in terms of experience as against the manipulative claims of pop, populist, or mass market ideologies. That is the authority one senses, for example, in Jean Toomer's *Cane*, at those moments when the experience of the rural South overwhelms the voice of the urban black and begins to speak through him. And that is why the essentially solipsistic form of *One Hundred Years of Solitude* is perfect: Macondo is precisely not history, however much of the historical it may include, but a construction of the way people believe themselves to be. Books in this Faulknerian mode tend to be oracular because a people's version of itself, not in bondage to history, has the power to affect the future. In Gilbert Sorrentino's *Mulligan Stew*, on the other hand, you get the Joycean situation of the use of epic, traditional reference by means of which contemporary experience is amplified and put in context. Sorrentino's novel, through Joyce and Flann O'Brien, uses the authority of the epic tradition specifically and the cultural tradition in general. It is a book which, in the epic manner, intends a certain scope, though its style is mock epic, resulting in an oddly modest exercise despite its sprawl. *Ulysses* and *Finnegans Wake* have the dimensions of an attempt at cultural summation that makes *Mulligan* look like a local joke in the mode of *The Rape of the Lock*. But there is something moving in the attempt, especially in the way this innovative book only makes sense toward the end where it is most deeply embedded in the past. It is a formally untraditional novel whose only rationale is in the tradition it mocks, a tradition, moreover, that is extremely remote from the American present. Its synthesis, though it does not ring false, is cameo in all but size, limiting the contemporary authority of the narrative voice in order to invoke that of the past. An interesting, if much less successful, effort to establish a persuasive narrative point of view is Robert Nichols' recent utopian tetralogy, *Daily Lives in Nghsi-Altai*, which attempts to resurrect the omniscient voice through the authority of the sociopolitical collective. However, its tone of utopian irony ("wouldn't it be nice if it were so?") suggests a consciousness that cultural authority cannot be established by social fiat.

VI. The Autonomous Text

The reflexive text gives up the idea, finally, of a voice of authority speaking *through* the book. Textual self-reference makes it clear that authority can only reside in the text itself. Richard Brautigan has fun with the situation in a style that acknowledges the reality of the text as opposed to the reality of its subject. In Donald Barthelme's *The Dead Father*, there is no "big picture" to which the text can refer as its authority. In fact, that novel represents an attempt to move beyond the fragments in which Barthelme usually deals toward some form of synthesis, an attempt to reestablish the authority that died with the paternal force. As the novel tells us, the older generation is interested in the big picture, but the younger generation knows there is no big picture and therefore it's more interested in the frame. *The Dead Father* is an attempt to impose a frame on the chaos of experience in order to make sense of it. But if there is no "big picture" there can be no authoritative frame, and we are left with a novel in which the fragments are more powerful than the synthesis. With the loss of the frame and the authority of the frame, which is to say, the authority of the narrative, there comes a loss of the authority of the narrator, and at that phase one begins to hear not only about the death of the novel but also about the death of the author. The author who, failing all else, was presumed to be the source and guarantor of the integrity of the text, turns out to have no such authority. The author becomes someone who, you might say, activates the process of language through the system of a given text, allowing the language to speak itself. Kenneth Gangemi's *Olt*, for example, represents an effective annihilation of the author in favor of the autonomy of found fragments. In the "constrictive" texts of the Oulipo group (Queneau, Calvino, Perec, Harry Matthews, among others) the writer's essential role is to formulate a rule or rules from which the text systematically unfolds—Perec's omission of the letter *e* from his novel *La Disparition*. The text is a preprogrammed system that generates itself. A related example is Burrough's manipulation of fragments in the cut-up method, heightening the reality of the text as a generative medium. In Daniel Spoerri's *An Anecdotal Topography of Chance*, the text is autonomous in that it is a system activated in particular ways depending on how the reader chooses to read it. To a certain extent, this is also true of Cortázar's *Hopscotch*.

VII. Docutext

A logical extension of the decreased importance of the narrator, and even of the author, is the kind of documentary text that we get in the books of Michael Ondaatje and Paul Metcalf. This technique derives its authority from actual use of the data, texts, and testimonies of the culture. It is a strategy that plays with what we consider to be the source of truth in the culture insofar as we acknowledge one at all, the truth of empirical observation. There are all sorts of variants of the documentary novel: faction, the nonfiction novel, the works of Tom Wolfe, Hunter Thompson, Doctorow, Mailer, and Capote. However, even given that there is always a certain amount of imagination in journalism and a certain amount of subjective interference in works supposedly based on empirical observation, the use of those forms in basically fictive integrations denies them the only kind of authority particular to them. The work of Metcalf and Ondaatje, as well as that of Burroughs, is more persuasive, in that it deals not with presumed "fact" but with manipulation of received texts. They leave the ambiguities of fact and observation to others and deal directly with language itself. This mode avoids the drawback of the novel of information of which Pynchon is the master, whose authority depends on the very American credulity about accumulation of data, as if truth and quantity are necessarily identical. The docutext also avoids or, at least, evades the mysteries of subjectivity that seem to terrify many American novelists, even though it might be argued that an investigation of consciousness is precisely the direction in which one must move when the sanctions for observation become ambiguous. In Metcalf, risks are limited by limiting the narrative situation to an ironic one in which collaged texts are left to comment on one another. The gain is in finding an apparent way to move beyond the reflexive, though it could be argued that what is sacrificed here is the original referent for the sake of a new linguistic integration twice removed from the data on which it is based.

Various other ways of moving out of the cul-de-sac of self-reference developed in the sixties and seventies. Burroughs' cut-up method, through collage, releases information in his materials that is unpremeditated and not manufactured by his own ego. Another method involves a kind of imprinting of phenomena in the manner of the sculptor Keinholz, or of Segal's plaster-casting of his models. Photo- or hyper-realism, however, like the *nouveau roman*, has its limits as statement. That the surface of the subject can never be reproduced by the surface of the composition about it, however "realistic," is a one-shot insight that cannot maintain the foreground long without referring—if not to the original subject—then to a contextual background developed by the composition. If the surface represents images from common experience, the background represents their metamorphosis by consciousness through language. In *The Death of the Novel and Other Stories*, I attempted, with intentional naivete, a new realism by taking imprints of "reality" with a tape recorder with varying combinations of such foreground/background relations in order to move beyond the impasse of narrative authority implied by the general increase in our consciousness of linguistic and narrative limitations. In fact, the variety and sophistication of the actual narrative attempts to meet this situation—as opposed to theories about it—thrives in the United States, not to mention the Americas, with a vigor unmatched by parallel developments in Europe. One of the components of so-called postmodernism is simply a move away from European models for narrative. On the other hand, our practical criticism lags behind developments in fiction, often seeming stubbornly simpleminded. Think of "moral fiction."

VIII. Process Text

One consequence of the breakdown of the narrative frame is to throw into question the matter of how a narrative should begin and end. A work of fiction, rather than being defined by the traditional beginning-middle-end kind of closure, might under the circumstances be considered as a process whose beginning and end are incidental rather than intrinsic to its form, and whose distinctive feature is the way it unfolds. Its continuity rather than its closure would define it. Such a work might, for example, take the form of a series, theme and variations, or systematized proliferation, any of which could end at any point after its essential mode had been established without fundamentally altering its character. A process text derives its authority in part by being able to acknowledge the reality of the processes of writing and reading beyond artifice, a narrative situation that is approached in, for example, *Malone Dies*. John Barth's well-known story, "A Self Recorded Fiction," is a witty and accurate parody of the text as a self-referential process. However, it seems to be based on the assumption that the basic authority for fiction is imitation of reality, which, once called into question, can only result in the text turning back on itself in the form of reflexive parody. Barth's response to this impasse is an admission and attempted exploitation of the situation, found in his essay "The Literature of Exhaustion," which in effect recommends that literature turn from imitation of reality to imitation of literature. This attempt to turn defeat into victory is based on an initial misapprehension of defeat. Fiction does not and cannot have the same sanctions as history or journalism. Critics who attack contemporary fiction for "self-consciousness" are really attacking its momentum toward increased consciousness of narrative as a medium. Increased consciousness provokes anxiety, but nevertheless that look in the mirror is part of the culture's impulse toward an increasingly intelligent proliferation of its own existence, part of our ongoing process of civilization. We not only need to know things, we also need to know that we know them and how we know them, questions of authority that contemporary fiction takes into account as do philosophy, science, linguistics, sociology, and other disciplines. If we admit the validity of an ongoing process of cultural creation, it would seem that the creative processes we have devised to that end have a certain validity in themselves. We can say then that the job of narrative fiction is not to record some preexisting reality but to contribute to the ongoing process of culture

building in and through the process of writing itself. The act
of narrative creation then assumes a fundamental authority
more or less embodied by particular examples, some of which
expose the essentials of process itself, as in the works of
Genet, or Raymond Federman.

IX. The Holy Book

Narrative fiction, unlike history or journalism, is about what
hasn't happened. Like religion, though in a different way, it
deals in faith. For the believer, "once upon a time" means,
"here is something that hasn't happened, but might." Fiction may falsify the past but it helps invent the future. In fact,
formally, all stories lead us into the future, into what is going
to happen. Narrative, by its very nature, is a process of what
happens next, and next, and next. Every novel is in the nature of prophecy in that it represents the projection of a future. But the essential trope of fiction is hypothesis, provisional supposition, a technique that requires suspension of
belief as well as of disbelief. Thus, if fiction deals in faith, it
also deals in skepticism, requiring the point of view of both
Sancho and Quijote. We have to take the projections of fiction, finally, on faith, but on faith tested by the challenges of
experience. If the sacred can be defined as faith in a particular course of events, as in our holy books, it might be said that
fiction turns the profane into the sacred in a process whose
authority derives from the continuous skeptical challenges of
common experience. So regarded, fiction might disclose the
potential for certain functions and rhetorical possibilities
long neglected by its European tradition and not to be found
in the recent dominant examples of Hemingway and Fitzger-
ald. The flow of experience can never be framed—it passes

and is gone. But the artifacts that art produces exist in an eddy of experience where they can be reexperienced, contemplated and re-visioned in the context of the reflexive mirrorings and reduplications of meditative consciousness. Repetition is an essential of literary art, from the pure repetition of metric in poetry to the re-creation and contemplation of experience that is fundamental to fiction. The incremental repetitions and re-visions of literary writing signify its existence in a realm continuous with the common flow of experience, but reflexively intensified, one that can avail itself of special forms and a special language.

Perhaps the authority of narrative writing at this point might profit from drawing on the powers of high rhetoric, of, for example, the Sublime, and on narrative effects ignored by our tradition of mimesis. Such techniques can summon up the intense affect required for the emotional integrations and disintegrations associated with matters of faith rather than with those of description and reportage. In moving into areas associated with the sacred text, such as parable, prayer, incantation, magic, prophecy, and myth of origin, in becoming a medium between individual and collective experience opposing the manipulations of the media, a medium that might serve as an oracular bridge to reconnect the profane with a sense of the sacred, the narrative might once more authenticate fiction as having some urgency other than the commercial. This is certainly one of the directions indicated in Joyce, especially in *Finnegans Wake*. But along with the repetitions of tradition in Joyce goes a corresponding iconoclasm, a profanation and dismemberment of tradition through collage. Collage is a technique for cutting up received texts in order to examine the possibility of new integrations, and so serves as a method for desacralization. Profanity, blasphemy, and desecration perform dark and necessary services in the holy book, moralists notwithstanding. They have the power, not to forge the uncreated conscience of the race, but to help uncreate the forged consciousness of the mass market, the mass media, the masses, or of whatever forces serve as mystification of the course of experience. The skepticism consequential to suspension of belief opens dangerous possibilities of change in belief. In places where art is taken seriously—Eastern Europe, France, Latin America, China, almost everywhere but in the Anglo-American tradition—artists have inherent political status because they are perceived as dealing with belief. The Anglo-American doctrine of willing suspension of disbelief neuters our narrative writing and confirms its inferiority and bondage to fact rather than its liberation in thought. Fiction has to lay claim to truth beyond that of data if it is to reinstate its authority in competition with the prestige of journalism and the high-flown journalism of mimesis. Journalism and history are oriented toward the present and past. It may be that the claim of fiction, incorporating as it does our attempt to reconcile our hopes with our fate, is on the future.

1984

Film Digression

Going to the movies. Down Graves End Avenue—now Mac-Donald—under the El past Malamud's delicatessen, location of *The Assistant*, to the Culver Theater Saturday afternoon with the kids. In the boondocks of Brooklyn, the early forties. Every Saturday a ritual in the flickering darkness. Initiation, via electronic ghosts, gigantic shadows, to reality. Because for us moving from traditional immigrant cultures into an America in process of redefining itself, reality was always elsewhere, and the Culver Theater, cheap, smelly, floor covered with Crackerjacks, was the authoritative elsewhere for eight-year-olds, spitting us out onto Graves End Avenue after three hours with irresistible pre-fab attitudes, ways to behave, things to want. There was no way to resist. My father always complains about movie prices because he can remember when they cost a nickel, and how he used to help Norma Talmadge with her homework so she could go hang around the Biograph Studio, my mother how her family forbade her to go for a screen test on grounds it was disreputable. But we, the kids, were surrounded, no resistance. Every

Saturday we were pulverized and remolded. I still recall that feeling of mental granulation after seeing a double feature. I feel it even now watching TV. The stupefaction of the mind adjusting to the energy and rhythms of the spreading electrosphere. We were the first generation not only dipped in the electronic bath, but left to swim, or sink, in the ambient technology of wave forms. There was, of course, radio. Soap operas, comedy shows, war news, the Lone Ranger and Dodger games. But the radio you could shut off, change the station. Once you entered the Culver, you were in an environment over which you had no control. A little like the theatre, but the theatre was Broadway. There was at least ten years between my first movie and my first Broadway show. Movies were on Broadway too, but they were also at the Culver and almost anywhere else you happened to be: recorded wave patterns, movable environments.

What did that mean, growing up in the electrosphere? It meant, for one thing, that we were surrounded by stories. Of course there were books, mostly comic books, image and word. I learned how to read with comic books. But they were stories told through images, the words were mostly dialogue. A lot like the movies, except the movies moved. That was the thing about movies and the radio, they kept moving past your mind like the scenery from a car, except you couldn't go back. They were irreversible and they had their own speed that you had to accommodate to, stories which in that way were a lot like life. And because of that quality, information in the electrosphere was a lot like stories, the anecdotal newsreels, *The March of Time,* current events as "developing stories," history as narrative, not retrospective narrative, not omniscient narrative, but history on the basis of incomplete developing information, the latest bulletins. History in process, as process. The war news on the radio in ongoing installments. This is not like reading *Pride and Prejudice*, or even Hemingway. The old novel, with its implications of depths and perfections, everything captured and understood once and for all, in a static and tightly woven texture for eternity. In the electrosphere there is no eternity. There is only infinity, everything always changing forever. There is no perfect, ultimate statement of anything, because there is no ultimate and no perfection. If it's not right the first time say it again, that might be a little closer, or one thing added to the next might get you there, but if you go back and revise, by the time you're done everything will have moved past you. You'll get a perfect statement of something that's already beside the point, the point being to keep up with the speed of your mind, which is most approximated by the speed of electricity. Growing up in the electrosphere you learn how to deal with speed, the speed at which information comes in at you, the speed of assimilating it, developing new integrations with it. This is what the movies teach you, to stay on the surface, to stay with the images and sounds as they move through your mind, to process strange streams of information and unfamiliar environments quickly into meaningful integrations, too much happening too quickly to be handled by discursive thought. Later, within the developing story there may be time for a playback or two, for what is traditionally known as "thought." Meanwhile, I'm too busy thinking to have time for thought. Thought is the province of the university, which is totally dedicated to playback, while outside the academy walls we're improvising on the basis of the ongoing, the arbitrary, the unforeseeable, that demands our constant invention.

A lot is made of the way movies have affected fiction via its techniques—montage, quick cuts, short scenes. But I'm talking about movies reinstituting story as a way of thinking.

The electrosphere has taught us, has required us, to narrate ourselves as we go along. We imagine ourselves as if we were on film or radio or TV because we have to imagine ourselves in terms of the way information comes in at us, and that image of ourselves in the media gives authority to our experience, makes it real, while at the same time the need for that reflection induces a kind of schizophrenia that in turn increases our need for media reflection to make our experience real. All media induce schizophrenia, increasing the need for feedback, in order to determine where between self and reflection the reality lies. Reflection leads to self-consciousness leads to reflection as thought. How can writing deal with this new, electrospheric narrative situation? And, in fact, why do we need writing to do it? Three techniques: collage, improvisation, and arbitrary form. Collage, of course, in the sense of montage, film not only uses but is the model for. But collage also in the sense the painters use it, the sense of Rauschenberg's use of the word "assemblage": a way of importing foreign material into the text, in whatever medium it may be. This film can do only with difficulty, while writing can use anything that can be coded in language or still image, through photograph, design, or quotation. Improvisation requires a supple medium—music, painting, or language. The more abstract the medium the easier to improvise, while movies are the most concrete and in a sense the most cumbersome of the media. And the only arbitrary limitation movies easily avail themselves of are the technological ones, while writing can impose any limitation it can invent in its self-consciousness. Henry Miller fast, improvisatory writing, Joyce collage, Raymond Roussell arbitrary form.

With these three techniques, perhaps, narrative writing can encounter the flow of the mind encountering the flood of experience in the electrosphere. In improvisation, the mind's language solos like speech without sound, like an ongoing sentence that forgets how it began, the mind's internal monologue which, even as it falsifies the past, invents the future. Not writing like speaking—Céline, Miller—but that speaking is like thinking. So writing as the written extension of all that mental jazz, recording the mind's ongoing music, like taping a saxophone solo. And collage is to get the stuff into it, the kitchen sink, the disparate, miscellaneous, random materials of experience, beyond the ungoing mental categories of what's acceptable, especially those of art and literature. And arbitrary form to constantly try to break down those categories, to force thought beyond what it already thinks, meaning beyond what it meant, to de-fab the pre-fab, mediating meditation into the unpremeditated. Thus narrative writing moving us into a fuller consciousness beyond the restrictive, if acute, diagrams of discursive thought, beyond its obsessive replay, with invention, fiction, being a sort of normal consequence of that ongoing solo that progressively questions the fact of the past in order to improvise the possibilities of the future, a dialogue there between the possible and the impossible to reclaim the impossible. Writing then as a movement into fuller consciousness, but writing also in its functions of memory and prophecy, word on page still unsurpassed in the technology of information retrieval, utterly different from the ephemeral improvisations of speaking and thinking. Writing as the most supple and powerful replay technology, and there its supreme advantage as the most self-conscious of forms, paradoxically more self-conscious even than thought in mind.

My own experience writing films persuades me that ideally they shouldn't be written. Films are not the writer's medium anyway. They're the director's medium or even, when you think of packaging, the producer's medium. Francis Ford

Coppola has constructed a system of filmmaking that could eventually do away with the written script. It involves faster retrieval of more information about recorded sounds and images, so that composition of the film can become a process of ongoing improvisation and revision as in writing. And in fact that is basically how a script is written and rewritten, but over a long period of time, and time-lag is what Coppola's system avoids, making filmmaking that much more the director's medium. Composition, recording, and editing are all almost simultaneous, so the making of the film gets very close to the process of thinking about it by the director, an extension of his thought process. Thus in terms of creative process, filmmaking begins to approach the suppleness of writing. In theory this should allow for the creation of more various and original work, less limited by the technology of the medium. From my point of view as a writer, this is a relief in a way. Films are involved with images and ideas; initially they have little to do with writing or language. I think what we are going to see, in fact, is a process in which the various media will essentialize themselves on the basis of technology. One sign of this is that within the various media the genres are beginning to break down and the forms are beginning to combine and essentialize what a particular medium can technologically best do. So, for example, the written media—poetry, fiction, nonfiction, journalism—have over the last ten or fifteen years begun to combine in various new and interesting integrations, aiming I would guess toward forms more appropriate to an essentialized writing technology. Its possibilities are not therefore narrowed, but expanded with the help of new technological developments like tape recording, xeroxing, print variable and computerized typewriters, word processing, photo-offset and computerized printing. Genre is traditional, medium is technological. We live in a technological not a traditional culture. So we will soon have, apparently, movies without scripts, so that the visual becomes visual and the written written, a kind of separating out of the media via the centrifugal energy of technological evolution and the intellectual revolution that is both its cause and effect. The breakdown of genre will be accompanied by an increasing definition of media, and we may end up with a series of more and more highly defined media which will themselves become principles of composition in the sense that the genres have been.

I see a tendency for the media to become increasingly abstract so that they become more direct extensions of thinking. Language may polarize increasingly into writing and speaking, for example, with speech language facilitated more and more by the tape recorder, by language spoken over the media, and by the relatively new tendency to read poetry out loud rather than assuming its real location is on the page. Written language may have less and less to do with speech and more and more to do with the rhythms of the mind itself. Writing so polarized may become increasingly concrete, more word on page, more written. But this process of concentration should also allow for more abstraction. The more concrete, the more a thing-in-itself the symbol, the more abstract information it can carry. When the meaning of a symbol is reduced to "degree zero," that is when it has only formal meaning, it is most powerful as a carrier of information. A digital computer is more powerful than an analogical computer because it stores information in terms of a yes/no code as opposed to an imitative code. A yes or no indication is more simple and carries less meaning in itself than an analogical indication, and so can carry more information. The computer chip may become the model for abstracting and reproducing information, and perhaps creating and communicating directly through the computer will be the ultimate medium, into which one might feed data that can be fed back in a variety of narrative forms, written, visual, oral, all of them at once, or in some form that bypasses the senses altogether, feeding directly into the brain, having the embodiment, say, of something like a waking dream.

In any case, Coppola's system works with computerized signals, and in fact bypasses direct, sensuous, analogical recording and goes instead to signals on tape. This is something like the way music is now being recorded, with digital signals instead of analogical imitation of the sound. In both cases the principle holds: because the system is more abstract, it can record more information in a more manipulable way. The more abstract the recording of information, the more concrete the reproduction, the more sensuous, finally. Increased abstraction means the ability to store more information in a more retrievable form so that reproduction can be more detailed, precise and clear. At the same time, as I have said, Coppola's system makes his medium more like a direct extension of thinking, because it allows quicker feedback on more information. He doesn't have to wait months for the editing to see what the film is going to look like, for example. He can see what the film looks like right away and edit as he goes along. What was, in traditional filmmaking, a record of the thinking of the script writer, modified by the thinking of the actors and directors, and later, the editor, becomes now a form of narrative thinking for the director. He is recording his own thinking almost directly the way a writer does, the thinking that is involved in composition. As the painting is a recording of the artist's performance, writing of the writer's performance in composition, so now, as Coppola is aware, the film—more than a recording of an action—becomes the recording of the director's performance in composition. So the location of interest in the film must shift and essentialize. It becomes less an imitation of an action in the world and more a mode of visual narrative thinking. Its situation then is not unlike that of the contemporary novel. Yet it is less like writing and more itself, as film, as it ideally should be, bypassing writing because there is no longer a need for a script. On the other hand writing, in the contemporary narrative, more and more bypasses simulation of image, also known traditionally as description. Writing need no longer try to make the reader see, but instead deals in concrete bits of information which the reader may translate into a wide variety of reference: the sky is blue, the baby died. While the language of film becomes more and more visual, depending less on language cues. All of this is interesting not only in terms of where these arts are going but in trying to arrive at what their natures are considering their technology.

But we are not going back to silent film. What is the relation of film and language, image and word? To what extent can we leave language behind and communicate through images? Images, still or moving, can sometimes communicate more information more easily and quickly than language. Take roadsigns, for example, when information is coded as image, as opposed to saying on a sign that there might be a locomotive coming around the curve, look out. But the concreteness and immediacy of the image is also its limitation. Images are too specific to comprise a flexible mode of communication. A picture of a locomotive remains, in referent, a picture of a locomotive. Context might expand its reference some, or even a given tradition, but finally it is too cumbersome as a signifier. Image can be used in various ways to modify meaning in a written text. But though it may be true that a picture is worth a thousand words, a thousand words can be recombined in thousands of ways to denote thousands of meanings, while the denotation of the picture can only remain the denotation of the picture. Unless the context can be changed. And there may lie the clue to the use of language in film. Even a sparing use of language, as with a single word caption at the bottom of a cartoon, for example, can give the contextual information necessary to shift contexts, to multiply meanings, to make film a far more complex and supple medium.

This points to the use of the soundtrack in general of course, through sounds and music as well as language, and it seems to imply that film is a much more language-dependent art than writing is image-dependent, or even that film can only exist as a rather limited and stunted medium without use of words. Talk about the "language" of film may imply a state to which it aspires but at which it can never arrive, unlike theater, which does not deal in images, or painting, which deals only in images. Perhaps one of the models for film should be comic books (note the recent *Superman*), a medium that also proceeds frame by frame, the difference being that while comic books deal with written language film deals with spoken language: written language and image versus spoken langauge and image. In comic books the equivalent of the soundtrack would be the words written in the balloons, but there is no equivalent in film of the narrative material in the captions. This suggests that in order to exploit the maximum potential of film, the use of subtitles should be reinstituted, along with the soundtrack. That side of language which proceeds through the graphics of writing would seem a natural complement to a visual art, especially since writing is one of the most pervasive objects in our culture. This of course has been recognized by the many painters who, since the Cubists or, to speak of another stage of development, since Robert Indiana, have been incorporating written language as part of their subject.

Written language in film could serve (as in Godard) multiple purposes—in the form of subtitles, for example—not only to enrich the meaning of the continuum of images, but also to remind the audience of the artifice of the medium, and thus, in a Brechtian sense, to break the usually hypnotic relation between medium and viewer that amounts to a form of mind control, as opposed to that liberation and expansion of consciousness which seems to me characteristic of contemporary art at its best. For this purpose, in fact, why limit use of written language in films to subtitles? Why not lay the language on the frame in whatever position it seems most appropriate? On a vertical column along one side, say, as in Japanese painting, or scattered through the frame, randomly, or in graphic design that might itself enhance visual significance. Furthermore the contrast between writing on the frame and writing in the frame, that is to say, photographs of writing, might set up an interesting dialectic among the levels at which we engage in discourse, especially in terms of the authority of the various levels. For example a subtitle on a photograph would have more authority than a photograph of a subtitle. Why? And might not this lead us to the conclusion that the authority of the frame is finally technological rather than ideological, a state of affairs which, once conscious, we might then wish to subvert. Political and ideological consequences of the technology of the moving image are not negligible. Given their capability for inducing near-hypnosis, film and television are undoubtedly the most powerful techniques in the mass technology of mind control. Assuming we want to deprogram ourselves, it is important to remember that maximum consciousness means minimum control. Theoretically, and for similar purposes, we might also make use, on the surface of the film and the frame, of the graphic techniques used by such film painters as Brakhage. At the level of soundtrack, voice-overs could be used to create another stratum of meaning as opposed to that projected by the images and the speech continuous with the images; that is, voice-overs could create a discontinuity between language and image.

What should images sound like, what should words look like? These are the questions we have been asking, and they make sense only with film, which, even essentialized, remains a composite form. In general, however, the way words look should be given more attention than it normally gets. We're talking about writing. Writing is by definition a graphic entity, and is very different from speech, which is purely sonic. In an essentialized form of writing, words should no more have a sound than images should. Speech rhythms are interesting in writing only because they are closer to the rhythms of the mind than textual syntax usually is. The point of an essentialized writing is to be abstract enough to bypass speech and get directly into an extension of the process of thinking. Tape recording is a case in point. Tape recording is interesting because it breaks free more easily of the rules and categories of written language into a more flexible language, which, however, remains mere talk until you get it on the page. Talk is talk, no matter what kind of talk, we're all used to it. To its rhythms, to its suppleness, to its communicative immediacy, and to the negligible value we attribute to it, justly, in comparison with writing or thinking—just talk. Only on the page does electronically recorded speech of any kind acquire the power of writing. On the page where first of all it gains a revolutionary thrust as opposed to official syntax, where its superficiality—that is to say the way recording keeps language to its surface in the same way that film does because of its movement—does not allow us to dwell, to sink into the culture's prefabricated profundities, only on the page does that surface quality become significant, a way of saying that however much the word may resound with associative and etymological resonances it is still fundamentally a mark on a page, an image on a surface, a visually concrete manifestation whose power of abstraction comes from the fact that it is a real object in the same sense that a computer chip is a real object.

Thus one of the jobs of the essential writer is to clear words of their associative and etymological meanings in the same way you might erase information from a computer chip, erasing meaning until you arrive at essential form, essential structure on a larger scale, which then becomes available for the creation of new meaning. This accounts for the otherwise inexplicable power of Gertrude Stein's nonsense, for example, or the efficacy of Burroughs' cut-up method. Burroughs says,

The study of hieroglyphic language shows us that the word is an image . . . the written word as an image. However, there is an important difference between a hieroglyphic and a syllabic language. If I held up a sign with the word "rose" written on it, and you read that sign, you will be forced to repeat the word "rose" to yourself. If I show you a picture of a rose, you do not have to repeat the word. You can register the image in silence. A syllabic language forces you to verbalize in auditory patterns. A hieroglyphic language does not.[1]

The word has to be severed from its relations with the auditory world. We are no longer a culture of mouth readers. We no longer have the time to shape the words with our lips as we read. Can we afford a language whose power is so attenuated? Speed reading won't do the trick. But the very phenomenon of speed reading, its very popularity, is instructive, as well as what happens when you read rapidly. In speed reading you pick out the major features of the message and try to ignore the details. The details are there at another level if you wish to go back or if you wish to slow down at a certain point. Why not score written language so that this kind of reading becomes not an imposition on a writing meant to be read in another way, but a way of maximizing the power of language showing us how to read, giving us cues for reading, in the most effective way. Why, for example, have print moving from left to right left to right in a solid block down to the end of the page? Why not break up the page so that the important features are written, let's say, in isolation or in larger type or both, so that the details are there in blocks of smaller print if you wish to read them. Why stick with grammatical syntax where fragments or run-ons might be more effective? Why not use a picture or a graphic image when it might communicate better, that is to say, faster and more? Why not reinstitute calligraphy as the most flexible of written forms, which now, as reproducible as print through xerography and offset, could become a mass medium?

Writers should do everything they can to release words from their normal contexts and associations, to make them available for creative use. In so doing we will rediscover the magic of language in a demystified and practical form. The word treated as literal thing creates new configurations that we then notice or create in the world, the way mathematicians create, on the basis of pure formal elegance, equations that are then found to describe previously unknown phenomena in the world. Or like a Cubist portrait that its subject comes to resemble (Gertrude Stein: "It doesn't look like me"; Picasso: "It will."). Collage, assemblage, montage are techiques that allow words and images to be brought into new contexts and new combinations, in which old meanings are lost and new ones are created. Montage is basic to the vocabulary of film and assemblage important to that of painting. Collage has obviously been basic to the vocabulary of creative language throughout the twentieth century, to the point where now we might even begin to think of it not so much as a dated technique but a principle basic to our language, and therefore available for further development. The collaging together of all sorts of graphic signs, images, photographs, along with words, in a more fluid and dynamic language integration seems a distinct possibility. And if electronics discovers a technique (through a laser disc system perhaps) might it not also be possible to incorporate the moving image?

The technology of the page is still more powerful than any other, including that of the computer, for communicative and creative purposes in language because of the page's "retrieval system," scanning, paging, availability visually of information through simple eye movement on any page in any order. What about an electronic scroll that might heighten some of these characteristics, one that could store more information in much less space much more cheaply than book production, whose expense is becoming a barrier to its utility? What about a scroll whose configuration could be changed at need for purposes, for example, of examining a macrosection projected into a large broadsheet or, at the other pole, could be broken down into fiche for detailed examination of another kind, fiche that could contain segments of information of any size, from paragraph to sentence to word to syllable? Suppose we could arrive at the electronic equivalent of a page with its concrete material advantages and still under the control of the eye and the hand moving in any direction at any speed at the will of the reader, either in successive stills or in controllable motion depending on the pace and purpose desired? Such options are now available on good word processors. Here film and television are both the models and the means of investigation. What about an improved version of written words, finally, one that breaks away from the sonic base of syllabification on the one hand but does not move into the cumbersome concretions of hieroglyphs on the other, a new calligraphy, a line, say, that curves and telescopes and accordions on the basis of a frequency system, music without sound, Mallarmé's musician of silence bypassing the senses as much as possible to address the mind more directly: "Reading creates a solitary, tacit concert played in the mind, which grasps its meaning through the slightest vibration. . . . Poetry close to the idea is music par excellence."

Here we stop talking about any one of the media as a separate entity, but invoking as we have, painting, film, television and music, as well as written and spoken language, we grope, as many artists now do, toward a fundamental change in language itself, growing out of and creating a fundamental change in the culture, which from this point of view at least, makes talking about film in isolation seem trivial, if not impossible.

1985

The Finnegan Digression

went down trucking
to the blah blah   G
zork uh uuh   E
onna saddy nite   N
and why not   R
looka me ma ahma   E
vant gard a sperry
mentalist
w
  h
    e
      e
        e
          e
      but to
return to the nar
was there a nar uh yes
so I was out berg wat
chin uno dio glasses

What is everyone everywhere all the time?
Finnegans Wake. The funnymental novel
of our error.

What is it: myth, dream, vision, joke?
The content of multiple myth (including
the private myth of James Joyce in person).
The techniques of dream. The omniscience
of vision. The tone of a joke. A sacre-
ligious joke. *The Bible,* starring
James Joyce as God the Father paring his
fingernails on the chamberpot while he makes.
Makes what? His mock-epic of creation in
one movement, bowel, macrocosm through
Mickrocosm. A dirty joke? It always
is. Is the novel out of ordure? Dream,
vision, joke? All of these? None of
these? Art is finally art, not second-
hand life. A record of creation (and
all of creation) is a bible. And a
bible is a book. And a book is just a
book. An edition to creation. Break

train on thisyere two
f two faced dickey
and this was pitt
pittsburg mind yo
where they ain't
minds me of the t
went out with Duk
Dukakis Dooky we
called him lookin
fer the cacabird
left Port Moresby
at 2 inna AM and
made a b line for
the outback assho
o' creation old
sport dodging kan
garoos all the wa
back to the neoli
thic or pleistoci
ne yet well seems
only way to shoot
down a cacabird
is with stale
matzoballs that
Dooky ordered spe
cial from Rapopor
ts I tella you
this man stop at
nothing senor one
time traveling wi
a french pimp in
the Yucatan got a
terrible yen for
a blow job surrou
nded by jaguar an
butterfly you und
erstand well off
goes the pimp into

down restrictive ideas of fiction;
suggest concrete reality of book as
artifact.

E   What does it mean?
X   L A X What do you do when the rational
P   mind is constipated? You give it an
L   enigma. A statement so total it becomes
I   totally ambiguous. Babel = babble. Who
C   knows what will come out? The diarrhea
A   of criticism, explaining. Or the pleasure
T   of letting go, of not explaining, the lux-
I   ury of not having to understand everything.
O   Order becomes ordure—it stinks. Drop
N   it. Play around with it. Play becomes
     serious—a new order. Life is no joke.
     You can't win. Winagains Fake. The best
     you can do is enigma, puzzle, indetermin-
     acy. That's life. Back to enigma means
     back to life. Winagainst Fate.

     Finnegans Fake: is it real?
VS   It's not imitation. It's life in
EI   process, thought in process, process
RM   in process. But not real life—it's
YI   static: the more it changes the more
L   it says the same. If it moves it's
I   alive, if it stays still it's art.
T   If it does both it's Finnegans Wake.
U   It's a fake. But it inCORPorates. A
D   symbol indicates, a pun inCORPorates.
E   Some business. Is this corpse dead?
     Wake up. Similitude? Very.

C   Who's in it?
H   Don't be a character. Less definition
A   = more fluidity. Keep up with change.

the bush an next	R	Everything changes into everything else.
thing you know he	A	(Not self consciousness but multiple
turns up at Port	C	consciousness, multiple alternatives.
Huron with letter	T	Not individual but general. Mythic.)
from Michele Debr	E	From the cul du sac of life to the sac du
ay turns out he's	R	cul of the Wake.
an agent name of		
I. Bitchakokoff	T	
brain granulated	I	What time is it?
by voyage but ton	M	All the time. Now. And always. = mythic.
gue still in chee	E	(Linear? circular? random? interconnection?
k his or someone	S	a network?)
elses haha il	E	What comes next?
faut pas tousser	Q	Everything. And nothing (simultaneity in
sur l'escalier he	U	a continuous present). Plot counterplot.
used to say also	E	Pattern destroys sequence and tends
weivel weg nach	N	toward the concretions of the plastic
der schloss well	C	arts. Not sequence but interconnection.
turns out certain	E	A new ordure?
dialects of demo		
tic Afrikaans tha	N	Yes or no?
mean ladies crapp	N O	Not either/or, but/and. Indeterminate
er get the scene	E V	meaning = multiple possibility. Don't
blug zork well I	WE	negate, include. Synthesize, don't
was told he was a	L	anal lies. Simultaneous multiplicity.
charming swine bu		Say yes. Anyone can do it. It's a dead
turn out he wasn'		end that implies a new beginning, aWAKE.
t charming prego		
urp outrageous my	L	What's it made of?
dear suked over b	A	Words. Not narrative. Not description.
a tamarind tree y	N	Not observation. Not characterization.
darn and now to t	G	Not comment. Not detail. Words. The
a ttack tic attic	U	river rather than its containing banks,
webby old bottles	A	the water rather than its course, which
dead love notes o	G	is in any case circular. The medium
costumes granpa	E	itself, language, words as concrete
brain granulated		objects. A cure for schizophrenia:
by voyage at end		no more division between abstraction

waving cane I tel
you boy we're not
going to stand fo
this kinda thing
or sit still eith
we let these pimp
behing the scenes
un hinge the scen
take all apart wh
to lose all die a
in end in end tha
the sad the sadde
st take a stand r
rip their balls o
before too late
Bitchakok Dooky b
fore you know they
camping in you ba
the sad sadist he used to b
e called did awful things
but they always depressed h
im still good typ to have a
long on a birding trip if y
know what good for you used
to go out with granpa and
Dooky when a boy one time
stirred up a pack of cacas
roosting in a tamarind grov
e well such a shitstrom the
hit us with in two secs we
were grovelling up to our
knees in that grove I won't
soon for get grovlin ina gr
ove gorlin ina grove grovli
nina grove just you and me
underneath the tamarind tre
thankyou was good practice
for the jungle though it wa

and sensation, thinking and feeling.
Word as magic. Language is a thing to
be seen and heard, is real, not facsimile.
Back to expressive utterance and
immediate apprehension in metaphor—
that's real too, as real as the news.
Wake language is totally particularized
in a given context, totally itself, yet
it enlarges reality, discovers reality,
maybe creates reality. New language
connections = new reality connections.
The Word gives us life.

(How about a Wake language
whose frame of reference is
not fundament ally historical
but open to common experience
not committed to the black hole
of the dead end of the closed
circle of simultaneity but part
of the endless unpredictable river of sequence :concretion over
abstraction/ contemplation over
information/ esthetic over util-
itarian/ multilingual/ multi-
referential/ allusive/ assoc-
iative/ puns/ doubletalk/ scat
talk/ coinage/ portmanteau/ as
immediate as babytalk/ that
expresses not only the reality
of the head but that of the
whole body its feeling energies
needs sensations. Language is also
speech, speech is voice, voice
is of the body. A wake is all
about a body)?

full of of butterfly and
wild swine took along a por
ter name Debray reputed cou
charm a wild swine at thirty
yards unfortunately the but
terfly got him fofe eve re
ached the swine country butterly in that area particularly
ferocious millions of them floating a air currents like
flotsam in sargasso kill a men in seconds by brushing the
air away from him with their wings still not a bad way to
go monsieur et dames is it not urp scusa serve me right
for gobblin the matzoballs leavin us in jeapordous situation
o where is the twofaced dickey now or the red breasted
harris for that matter birds birds nothing but birds birds
to the end of it time to take a stand say gramps brain
granulated by voyage naught to lose he took one saw a bird
fly out of his mouth a soft grey brown one was that his
soul always something to lose sad rip their balls off
haf kaf and now its a titmouse out into the air as his
face says o not duk bitchstand for and now a junco appears
on his lower lip peers around flies off blug zork and now
a humbird rockets twixt his dessicate lips his wrinkled
old puss much chapfallen urp and now an owl and he chokes
on the owl see way I figure it always begins the same way
always ends the same way its whats in between what counts
well anyway there not too much you can say about it except
that it goes on it goes on it goes on except when it dont
that was in pittsburgh I believe a big turk truckin town
on a count a the big sperry plant there working with
pscyic phenom 200psychis there at one time using them for
navigation in wwII and enemy detection with implanted gyroscopes kept on course asad thing to see their was in
particular this turk name of asad birds flying out his
mouth brain granulated by voyage surround dead by jaguar

What would you do with it?
Play with it.
Joyce did.

What would you have then?
Funnagain.

1980

II. Cross Examination

The Interrogators

Joe David Bellamy—Ithaca, New York, 1970
James Nagle—Boston, Massachusetts, 1977
Charlotte Meyer—Buffalo, New York, 1979
Larry McCaffery—Buffalo, New York, 1981
Patrick Lavallé—Paris, France, 1981
Zoltán Abádi-Nagy—Debrecen, Hungary, 1982
Jerzy Kutnik—Lublin, Poland, 1982

Larry McCaffery: Why don't you [write autobiography]?

Sukenick: Because autobiography isn't that interesting. I am involved in actively re-creating my life, not simply recording my past.

McCaffery: When you say that autobiographies aren't interesting, do you mean in a formal sense? Or simply that it's a lesser form because you're recording events, rather than imagining them?

Sukenick: Both, actually. It's not interesting in a formal sense, and it's not interesting from the point of view of the data involved. I mean, who cares? You yourself care, but of what public interest is that data compared to what happened to Marco Polo or any fairly adventurous traveler or soldier of fortune? It's just of no intrinsic interest, and for that reason most autobiographies are really a kind of forgettable escape reading. That book *Papillon* is a good example of a wonderful read on that level, but I totally forgot it the minute I closed it. It was trivial.

McCaffery: But your fiction—especially your early fiction, such as *Up* and some of the stories in *The Death of the Novel*—has a lot of trappings of autobiographical fiction. Why did you use yourself as a literary character so often in those books?

Sukenick: Part of what I was doing then was just trying to get into an honest writing position. At a time when the whole question of whether fiction can say anything true becomes problematic, you can at least get yourself into a position where you can say, "Well, at least I can say something about my own experience anyway, directly, without making anything up." Of course, the challenge and conscious paradox there is that no matter how hard you try to get down the data as they literally are, there are almost no literal data. They are always filtered through the creative mind, even if that mind happens to belong to the person from whom the life data has come. You can see this idea pretty clearly in my story "Momentum," which begins, in effect, "I want to get the story down just as it happened on the tape recorder." And then, of course, it turns out that you can't do this. You should always *try*, though, to capture the data of reality.

But the whole idea of mimesis having been challenged, in my opinion successfully, there are two alternatives. The first is the one that Barth took, the retreat into literature. And I think that, despite all his talent and intellectual gifts, this was the wrong move for him; his works have gotten predictably claustrophobic. Barth's tack was to say that there is always the intervention of interpretation of some kind, so that you could never get at the "real data." So instead of talking about the data, he took the position—simply expressed in that essay, "The Literature of Exhaustion," which he published so long ago now—that since you are always looking at those data of experience through the interpreting mind, they are, in effect, *already interpreted*. No matter how you come at "reality," it is already interpreted before the fact. Then what you do is move into the interpretations and deal with the *interpretations*, not with reality, because that's what the really acute artist realizes he's dealing with. You become, then, a connoisseur of fiction, the expert in measuring and collecting and judging between and making distinctions among fictions. The other direction was to propose to yourself that fiction could tell some truth beyond your personal vision and beyond literature itself. I'm anti-mythic or post-mythic. You can't make up myth.

McCaffery: I take it from what you say about Barth that you feel you followed the second direction.

Sukenick: Yes, Barth's position—which I think is also Gass's and Coover's position—is one I've never agreed with.

My feeling is that you have always to move in the direction of the data of experience in "reality," whatever the chances that you can't do this. There's a line in Handke's *A Sorrow Beyond Dreams* where he talks about the effort to investigate and develop the psychology of a character—in this case, of his mom—and he says that he realizes he can't do it, that he can never successfully arrive at the reality of that character. But at the same time he says that you have to try. I think that's true: you have to try, because it is only in making that effort to deal with those data that you finally create a legitimate fiction. In other words, you don't create a legitimate fiction merely by dealing with other fictions. One of the main purposes of really good writing is to destroy other really good writing, to destroy all the old concepts and formulas that come out of the best of the past. You should destroy them lovingly and with great consciousness and awareness of them, but always with the end in mind of getting beyond them again. And knowing that they were also trying to do the same kind of thing.

McCaffery: I take it that your main goal in deconstructing these prior fictions is this process of "getting beyond." Otherwise you'd seem to be basically engaged in a similar kind of fiction-exploring—or destroying—game that Barth, Borges, and some of the other writers are playing.

Sukenick: But is what I was describing really deconstruction? If I were just deconstructing, that would be staying at the level of fictions. What I'm after is to deconstruct *not* back to other constructs, the way Barth does, but *to what lies beyond constructs*.

McCaffery: In your Wallace Stevens book, you have a passage that is frequently cited when critics talk about this issue: "The mind orders reality not by imposing ideas on it but by discovering significant relationships within it, as the artist abstracts and composes the elements of reality in significant integrations that are works of art." What this suggests to me is something very important: that there are significant relationships in reality that can be *discovered*, not merely invented and then applied.

Sukenick: No matter how much things are interpreted beforehand, there are still some kinds of data there. The main one is death, or maybe the main one is birth and the second is death, with a lot of others in between that are experientially there. It's not as if we're confronting a blank space. There's things out there that are undeniable and you have to find some way of dealing with them. There's an interaction going on between language and those data in which the effort is to get rid of old language formulas. What seems to happen is that you break down the language and, as you break down the language, since language can't be broken down any more than consciousness can (you can't confront a total blank, either in language or in your mind, unless you're dead or in a coma), you hope that language will break open and offer the opportunity to make new organizations that are appropriate to new situations out there. I'm not going to argue that language makes any direct contact with reality, but I think there's a changing metaphoric contact with reality, and the only way that change can occur is by breaking down the old fictions, the old constructs. When that happens I think you open up a new space. It's like cutting a log in a new direction: a new grain opens up, literally a new content appears when you cut something in a new way from the way it usually gets cut. You see different things; words then begin to surrender their meanings in different ways and begin to reveal all that huge amount of accumulated wisdom that language contains from the whole history of the culture.

McCaffery: Is this one of the sources, then, of your obvious interest in wordplay, puns, pangrams, and other language games? I mean, do these devices help the author with this process of opening up new spaces with language, forcing the words to yield new complexities and meanings?

Sukenick: Precisely. Language play releases the possibility of meaning that is inherent in language, that is built up in it through tradition. The wisdom of language only reveals itself, oddly, when you break it down. It's like breaking open a piece of fruit—if you can find a way of cracking it open, you can find a way of releasing its content, its energy, its suggestiveness, its possibilities. But in order to do that you have to deform it, or transform it, through puns or through arbitrary devices of the kind that Raymond Roussel uses—through the imposition of odd schemes, non sequiturs, even through improvisation. You have to do that kind of peculiar manipulation of language in order to release its peculiar *power*. You may, in the process, manage to startle or surprise the reader, but the important thing is to surprise *yourself*, to get out of the premeditated.

McCaffery: Gombrich says somewhere that wordplay unleashes a "preconscious idea" for both reader and author.

Sukenick: The only problem I have with that is the word "preconscious." I wouldn't characterize this process as preconscious at all. I would rather use the word "nonexistent." It's not as if it were there already in your consciousness; on the contrary, it's something that is totally beyond your consciousness, that you bring into your consciousness in that way, that you *create in language*. Of course, it can work both ways, the way that Freud used puns to reveal the unconscious. But *Finnegans Wake* uses wordplay in both ways: it reveals the unconscious and opens up the multiplicity of history that exists in language; and perhaps accidentally, as an inevitable increment given the way Joyce was writing, it had the effect of bringing into consciousness information that could not otherwise have been reached, information that was neither in history nor in the unconscious. It was totally new information.

McCaffery: I'm interested in what you meant just a minute ago when you said that your approach was seeking a truth "beyond literature." What is the nature of such a truth?

Sukenick: There is experience beyond language. There are things that go on in the sensorium of the body that are prelinguistic—and also postlinguistic—and that may or may not get into the language system. There is a whole chain of these "feelings" in the sense of what you experience when somebody touches you or kicks you. And that feeling registers in varying ways. For instance, it seems as if people are amnesiacs about pain once it's over, so I don't know what form pain really takes in the language system. There are probably lots of things that you feel physically that don't get into the language system. Then there's that other sense of feeling—feeling/emotion—and there is a gradation here. That is, bodily feeling turns into feeling/emotion; and of course the basic physical feelings turn into emotions most easily. Maybe pain and fear, or pain turning into fear, are the best examples.

McCaffery: And sex.

Sukenick: Yes. In a way, sex is the most of all, because it is pleasurable and desired. The reason sex is so powerful is because it's where feeling turns into feelings more easily. That may be one of the reasons, come to think of it, for this explosion of sado-masochism that's been going on in some circles (maybe a lot of circles) in this country. It may be that there's a kind of perverse curiosity about getting beyond formulated emotions back to an undeniable *source* of emotion, if we can talk about emotions becoming worn out, conventionalized, and inappropriate. This may be the same sense we get in language or fictional forms—maybe the whole *root* of that may lie in the emotions; maybe we have this feeling that our emotional life is fossilized and that the way to get back to that authentic source of emotions may be to get back to that precise point where your emotions are totally out of control. Thus the idea of being *forced* to have pleasure becomes attractive. There is an apparent authenticity there, however desperate, because it is out of our conceptual control, out of our cultural control, out of our conventional control. *That*, for example, is experience beyond language as far as I'm concerned.

McCaffery: Is this one of the reasons why so many of your characters—especially in *98.6*—seem to relate to each other, both sexually and personally, through violence or other means of heightening their reactions? You seem to be suggesting that this is a product of the age, a response to all the things around us which try to deaden our reactions, to conventionalize them.

Sukenick: In *98.6* I was very unsympathetic to these tendencies. I diagnosed the culture as lapsing into sado-masochism and suggested this was a kind of sickness. The idea I had there was that power and sex had gotten confused. I think this is still true today—that power and sex, or violence and sex, are often confused in our culture—and that they shouldn't be.

McCaffery: Do you feel that you can learn about life from reading novels?

Sukenick: I have learned a great deal about life from fiction, especially the fiction of Henry James. But the thing is that the world is changing, there are new circumstances that demand new paradigms. And you can't control these new circumstances the way the realistic model wanted to. It's like trying to hold together an armful of large balls—something's going to pop out somewhere. The effort at control is hopeless. What you have to do—and I hope that my fiction is exemplary of this process—is to learn how your fiction can *be a part of the environment*, rather than trying to control it.

McCaffery: This has nothing to do with the fact that contemporary society may be more out of control than the reality of the nineteenth-century realist?

Sukenick: Maybe that voodoo I mention is always at work for the serious writer. What he's trying to do is control his experience in some way, cast a spell on it, find ways of dealing with it. And what he leaves *behind* becomes, maybe, a model for the reader. But if it's control the contemporary writer is after, I'd say he has to modify this view, because I don't think the model is now control.

McCaffery: What is the model?

Sukenick: I'd say *participation*.

McCaffery: I recall that in your story "The Birds" you have a passage about how wonderful birds are because they "carve shapes from nothing, decorate the silence, make melodious distinctions to distinguish one moment from the next." Should this be fiction's main role today—to serve as decoration, to create distinctions in a world which threatens to obliterate distinctions?

Sukenick: Of course, fiction has a lot of functions. One of them is simply to give pleasure. That line in "The Birds" is really about that direction in fiction. It's like the way music keeps time: not retentively but just taking note of it, varying it, articulating it, and making it pleasurable. That's one function of fiction, but it has dozens of others. People are always saying, "What's the political function of fiction, what's the this or that function?" But fiction is so basic that it has many different functions simultaneously, all the time. I mean, what would you say if someone asked you, "Hey, what's the function of your mind?" It's like that.

McCaffery: What are your views about the so-called Gass-Gardner debate about the "moral nature" of art? Do you take sides in this affair?

Sukenick: Great art—whatever that is, whatever we finally agree on as being the great texts—*acquires* a moral value because it becomes normative. It says, in effect, "This is what consciousness should be like." But it's a very broad kind of moral value. It's not issue oriented, you might say. Now it's quite possible that fiction can be issue oriented—it can talk about moral issues, it can talk about love affairs, it can talk about all sorts of subjects—but if we say that fiction must be moral in its outlooks, we are putting art on the same level as propaganda. In fact, what would Gardner do with a morally noxious writer like Céline, who is nevertheless great? There are immoralities at the level of subject matter that are overwhelmed by the broader moral concern of seeing a consciousness articulate itself in such incredibly eloquent terms. Just seeing this kind of access, this increase in consciousness that a mind like that of Céline gives to language as a form becomes, in itself, a moral consideration finally, although if you just had somebody you know die in a concentration camp, you wouldn't want to read his books.

On the other hand, I'm not in favor of Yale having given Pound the Bollingen Prize. That was a very bad thing to do *at that time*; it was morally coarse, a crude thing to do. There was an estheticism involved that was misfocused, because there was no way you could avoid at that point Pound's pro-fascist, anti-Semitic activities. To give him the Bollingen award amounted to social recognition and approval of that part of his writing. That is not to deny, of course, the larger value of Pound's writing. I wouldn't deny that remark made about modern art—was it by Flaubert?—"The only obligation of the writer is the morality of the right sensation." That's quite true, in terms of composition.

McCaffery: Why do you think this notion of the "play" of literature and language comes up so often these days? And why does it make so many people feel uneasy?

Sukenick: Literature *is* playful, like sex is. Literature is a pleasurable activity, and play is a component of many kinds of pleasure. Maybe that's the reason for people's uneasiness: despite all the talk about personal and sexual liberation, playfulness is still a kind of taboo that makes people nervous. There is nothing that enrages people more than the idea that an artist is narcissistic. But why is this? Should they care? So it's perhaps best to take the position that the novel should be narcissistic, maybe even more than it is.

There are, of course, other ways of answering this. One is to say that this type of literature is *not* narcissistic, that self-reflexivity is a path—maybe the only path—to greater consciousness. Every implicit step to increased consciousness has to be accompanied by some increase of *self*-consciousness, just as the scientist needs to perfect the tools of the experiment before he can get results that tell him something about reality.

McCaffery: On several occasions you've said in print, echoing Robbe-Grillet, that the main job of the modern writer is to teach the reader how to invent himself. Is this a justification for the kinds of metafictional, self-reflexive strategies you employ in your early work—and that writers like Coover, Gass, and Barth regularly use?

Sukenick: Yes, this approach is an investigation of the creative powers of the mind, of the imagination itself, and of language. Its aim is to make people super-conscious—as conscious as possible of the way the imagination inevitably helps to shape reality around the self. The reason that this kind of approach becomes so important today is because of the pressure of the media, which is nothing so much as the manipulation of the mass imagination, a sellout of individual experience. The media impose manipulative paradigms on individual experience, so that it is almost as if people don't have any individual experience—they only have what they see being presented on television. Of course, that's not literally true, but things move ominously in that direction all the time. So I figure that one of the things that art is supposed to do is to teach people how to defend their experience and prevent it from being stolen from them by showing them how to use their own imaginations against that manipulative imagination which is not in their own interest. Oh, I suppose that the media sometimes present things that are in the public's interest, but if so it's probably an accident. The tendencies of mass manipulation are primarily in the interest of politicians and corporations or the consumerist society, which have to make and sell things in order to survive. It's directed by the profit-making mechanism in our society. It's not for the benefit of the individual, although benefits may accidentially occur—you see, I'm not a complete pessimist about conglomeratism.

McCaffery: In a metafiction, then, the idea is that the writer becomes a kind of exemplary person who can respond to the world through his own imagination—not an imposed substitute—and hopefully invent something that is personal and meaningful.

Sukenick: Exactly. That's the crucial *political* function of the writer: to resist that sellout of individual experience. And that's why a writer with a very individual voice can make a lot of people nervous. Maybe this is one of the reasons why the Fiction Collective is always enraging some segment of the culture—because they are the most uncategorizable voices around. A slick writer can say all sorts of uncomfortable, rabid things. Norman Mailer can say, "Bring down the establishment"; and as long as he says this slickly, it will slip into the scene and take its place with all the other discourse. But if somebody is intentionally crude, uncategorizable, rough, disorganized and yet is felt to be a quality writer with something to say, that, even when narcissistic, can make people nervous.

McCaffery: In your fiction and criticism you repeatedly bring up the attractiveness of jazz as an analogy for your own process of literary creation, especially the improvisatory nature of jazz. What advantages does a truly improvisatory approach to writing have over the traditional approach, which emphasizes artistic *control* at every step of the writing process?

Sukenick: Improvisation releases you from old forms, stale thoughts, it releases things that are released only with difficulty on a psychological basis. It allows in surprising things that are creeping around on the edges of consciousness. It prevents you from writing clichéd formulas. It's a release, finally, a release of the imagination. Today, however, I think that the idea of improvisation itself has become a formula and it has gotten very slack as a result. The novel got tired of improvisation in the beginning of the '70s. At least it did for me. Presently I seem to be moving in the direction of formalism— the kind of formalism that I think Coover and Abish are using. Another example is the sort of thing Federman used in *The Voice in the Closet*, in which you simply impose a form on your materials, it not really mattering how this form was generated. Calvino does the same kind of thing in—what's that book?

McCaffery: *The Castle of Crossed Destinies?*

Sukenick: No, I'm thinking of *Invisible Cities*. But the important idea is that the *genesis of form* isn't important, whether it's traditional or untraditional. The important thing is to have a form. I would say, in fact, that for this approach you don't want to have a traditional form because there are too many associations with it already—in a way, the form is already exhausted. So a truly nontraditional form would probably be an arbitrary form. But then the interesting thing becomes to begin investigating the differences between different kinds of form. We have an interesting formal situation there. Perhaps writers will come up with some totally idiosyncratic forms that can be used only once—which is fine—or forms that other people may be able to pick up on and use again and again. If this occurs, maybe we'd have a more continuous formal tradition. I know that I'm continually drawn, by temperament, to use idiosyncratic forms.

McCaffery: When you're starting out with a book, or even when you're in the middle of it, do these kinds of generalizations occur to you? You know, "Improvisation isn't working, I need formal structures," that kind of thing?

Sukenick: No. Most of what I've been talking about I realized in retrospect. Who thinks of these things while working on a book? While you're working there is a kind of fruitful chaos and ignorance—at least that's the way I work and the way most people I know work. When I start out with a book, the last thing I want to know is what the book is going to be like when it's finished. This is a very painful and risky approach, though, because while you're working on the book it looks like you're dealing with failure. In fact, you *are* dealing with failure, right up until the moment when the book is a success. *If* it ever gets there. But until that moment the book is definitely a failure. This is a very floundering, uncomfortable feeling.

McCaffery: Doesn't *98.6* end with the phrase "another failure"?

Sukenick: Yes, and I believe in the idea of failure at various levels. A paradoxical but familiar situation exists in America these days, in which an artist may be authenticated by failure or ruined by success. So in a sense I don't want to write books that are successes or to write "great books" in the old sense. Also, to write a book that is a total success would be to write a book that is totally inhuman. The closest thing I can think of to this is *Finnegans Wake*. An analogous situation, although it's not as great a book, is Beckett's *The Lost Ones* because it's totally hermetic and quite perfect in its own way. But there's an intentional flaw in its whole scheme, a way out of the text's hermetic world. It has to do with Dante: the way out of the *Inferno* is through the Devil's asshole. It seems to me that in *The Lost Ones* there is some similar way out, some flaw of human nature that becomes a virtue, as the flaws in human nature sometimes do, simply because they're characteristic. Anyway, the kind of book I most want to write is the kind of book that *fails* back into the experience which it is about. It emerges—and re-merges—with this experience, having added itself to it. But I'm not interested in creating a book that remains in its own perfect sphere, apart from experience. My work has to cancel itself out to do what it is trying to do. It isn't trying to transcend experience, but is trying to add to experience.

McCaffery: Is there any aspect of writing you could isolate as being the most intriguing to you?

Sukenick: That makes me stop and think. There's a lot that is intriguing: the rhythm of the sentences, their sound, but probably what I find most interesting is the way I get into a fiction and it literally starts producing new experiences for me. It's like having a second life, simultaneously with the first one. Or it's like Wordsworth blanking out and having visions. So although I'm not a mystic at all, it's very exciting to see all that new experience coming at you out of your own mind, adding to your life.

McCaffery: Are there any other art forms—television, the cinema, perhaps recent trends in painting—that have affected your writing?

Sukenick: Abstract Expressionism seems to me to be the basic art movement of this half of the century because it was an investigation of the reality of art itself and established its reality in a non-puritan way. It got rid of illusion and all those other pejorative terms like "suspension of disbelief." Illusion traditionally is a pejorative term, yet it has always seemed in our tradition the center of art. So no wonder the puritans didn't like it. Abstract Expressionism got rid of that whole notion that art is apart from life, that it is something special which is siphoned or partitioned off from experience—art as a vampirelike entity that sucks the juices out of life and puts it into this esthetic place that is of greater value than life itself, and is put by millionaires into museums so that people can come in, look at it, and approve of themselves. That whole schizoid split between art and life was broken down in Abstract Expressionism by virtue of its discovery of a new locus of reality for art—it moved everything back to the act of creation, rather than the act of audience appreciation. It said that the reality of art is the reality of *making art*—everything comes from this, instead of taking the position that the reality of art is located in the act of receiving or appreciating it, something that denies or soft-pedals the process of creation. When you look at a work of Abstract Expressionism you're forced to remember that there was a hand there that created it. There is an attachment to life without any schizophrenia, without any alienation. Art therefore becomes a human act—you're forced to say to yourself, "This painting I'm looking at was done by a person," and take it on that basis. I hope that my fiction has applied some of these principles.

McCaffery: What you're talking about seems the opposite of the Jamesian or Joycean idea of the work of art with no creator present—the God paring his fingernails over a work.

Sukenick: Yes, and in fact Abstract Expressionism represented the sudden explosion or destruction of the modernist movement.

McCaffery: I agree—modernism seems to me to have emphasized the ability of the artist to put the discontinuous fragments of modern experience together into a work that could oppose our sense of chaos. You know, it offered a kind of example of unity and coherence to people who couldn't find these things anywhere else. But postmodern writers and painters seem to refuse to allow this to happen—they seem to want to remind us that reality is chaotic and discontinuous.

Sukenick: Yeah, an Abstract Expressionist painting is another fragment added to the pile, but it's an *intelligent addition*, not a transcendent object.

McCaffery: I've always thought that one of the most striking aspects of your fiction is your refusal to present your characters as consistent beings with identifiable traits. Rather, like clouds, your characters are always shifting into different shapes, different beings, with different names, contradictory attributes, and so on. Do you do this mainly to emphasize the difficulty—or even impossibility—of devising a unified notion of self?

Sukenick: If you drop the idea of imitation as the mainstay of fiction, then the idea that you need "characters" drops away pretty quickly. You realize that characterization is always simply a part of the text or part of the consciousness of the writer, depending on at what point you wish to start talk-

ing about character. Either way, it's a division of the whole
into a dialetical fragment. The whole consciousness breaks
up into its parts, and various energies can begin to flow because of that polarizing among the parts. The fragmentation
can then alter the parts, or the parts can be combined in different ways, and the final consequence can be that an alter-
ation can take place in the whole consciousness or the whole
text. In any case, that willful fragmentation of the ongoing
narrative—or of the ongoing experience of a given consciousness in the process of composition—creates energy, creates
detail. What goes on beneath the ordinary idea of characterization—having characters interact and conflict within a fictional world, for example—is really not very unlike the ordinary process of the mind in any inquiry about anything. In
this case, instead of the entities being concepts, ideas, symbols, points of view, they are called Frank, Mary, and Larry.
In both cases, the entities involved combine, recombine, split
up. They die, they loose validity, they gain a certain authenticity—all as a result of the larger argument of the text. More
and more, as the idea of imitation drops away, the necessity
for having these entities under the label of hard-and-fast,
well-rounded characters also drops away. You begin to realize that the process of characterization is the process of fragmentation and dialectic that the mind ordinarily pursues—
although this process is pursued within a particular context
and toward different ends than in, say, philosophy. Madame
Bovary represents one cluster of traits of the bourgeoisie,
Huck Finn represents one side of the split of the frontier,
Ahab and Moby Dick (is Moby Dick a character?) symbolize
something, and so on. So even traditional characterization
has always been doing this.

The other side of this—since I've only been talking about
the literary or textual side of this issue—is the sense I have

that individuals' personalities are becoming less and less important and less defined.

McCaffery: Do you mean less well-defined, more fragmented, in comparison, say, with people in the nineteenth century—the people represented in the great realist tradition?

Sukenick: Yeah, even compared to the kinds of characters I would see in my father's generation or especially my grandfather's generation, who were very august, aggressively rigid personalities. It seems that people now, for better or for worse and for good reasons usually, are less defined—more "laid back," as they say, "going with the flow" and all that. I'm using these clichés on purpose to show that people think about personality, even their own, in this way. I also like to believe that you can have a more flattened out, flowing, less rigidly defined personality that is still not necessarily uninvolved on its own terms.

McCaffery: Any theories about what's creating this change in personality structure?

Sukenick: It has something to do with the change in the methods of political and financial organization, and the methods of communication. Obviously, for example, all over the world societies are moving more in the direction of collectivization instead of individualism. It may well be that the age of individualism of Henry Ford and George Bernard Shaw is dying out, and that the social, political, and economic conditions that made that kind of definition possible—or even necessary and advantageous—are gone. Maybe it's the end of a process that began with the Renaissance. But this idea of pursuing a job or career, with the individual succeeding through conflict and struggle; the idea that character—which is what Undershaft in Shaw claims runs England—was the thing that saw you through that process and was its driving force, man's most essential untouchable element—all that has been eroded by the sense of collectivity, by the sense that people's character traits can be drastically changed by drugs, by brainwashing, by the interchangeability of people in corporate slots, by the rate at which information comes at us. It's just very difficult to absorb and respond to so much information while having a hardened, brittle personality circumference, as opposed to one that is porous.

Patrick Lavallé: What is "reality" in fiction?

Sukenick: We use to deal with the term reality in literature in a naïve way. However, some books put the quotidian reality into question. The first example I can think of historically is Hugo von Hoffmanstahl's "Letter to Lord Chandos," on the impressionists, a long story that questions everyday reality. It is a luxurious kind of upper middle class complaint you find in Hoffmanstahl: that everyday reality does not mean anything. You can find it in *La Nausée* of Sartre also. But for somebody whose life is a struggle every day this attitude is impossible because the pressure of reality is too heavy. You could say in a crude way that for the upper middle class life is not real enough but it is too real when you're poor. Someone like Raymond Roussel is beyond that question; he has an aristocratic point of view. For him reality seems to reside in form itself.

The important question is in fact: What is the authority for the validation of the work of art, where does it come from? For me, Roussel's work is important as a way of producing language that can invent reality. It is a way for language to validate itself. In the way I use the language, there is no question of imitating reality in the traditional sense of fiction. If anything, I would say that fiction falsifies reality. But on the other hand, simultaneously it reinvents it. It's that point where Roussel's methods become very interesting to me because invention is by definition something unforeseeable. Roussel suggests ways to get beyond preconception. I don't mean so much the particular ways he uses puns and so on, I don't particularly use that kind of method although I know Harry Mathews does along with the whole Oulippo group and their idea of constrictive form. For example, Mathews does something he calls a logarythm which is a kind of mechanical way of inventing phrases. The spirit of Roussel, that is, the spirit of the arbitrary is very important for me, as important as collage, or improvisation, as a technique for reducing preconceived formulation in my language in order to allow the release of the unpremeditated.

The fact that Roussel was engaged in pure linguistic invention is the important thing. It reflects a larger kind of phenomenon. In fact language does invent reality itself in a more remote way. In our tradition, language has become an extension of the mind, especially written language. It provides a medium of reflection that we meditate on and go back to. I am not talking of language in general but I am talking of writing specifically. It seems to me to be the best extension of thought that we have, the most direct way of deepening the process of thinking. For example in one of Saul Bellow's books, *Henderson the Rain King*, there is an episode where Henderson is in an airplane and he keeps thinking that first people dreamed about this and we are now doing it: flying. Invention is our thought crystallized in language, and then realized in terms of realities like the airplane. The culture is literally invented by the creation of language since it realizes itself through language. Roussel, by some lunatic sort of genius, like an idiot savant, manages to get at the very center of that process, and to show its importance.

Lavallé: Roussel's interest in scientific research and inventing machines functioning on the principles of language makes language itself into a machine that finally works and produces reality.

Sukenick: Now we have to speak about writing as a cybernetic phenomenon. It has something to do with the computer. There seems to be a movement in writing towards abstraction, away from imitation or representation. In physics, for example, we discovered that no exact representation of phenomena is possible at the atomic level for one reason: the observer gets in the way of what he's observing. The only possible manner of representation becomes a statistical one which is highly approximate. The connection between what used to be called reality and the mind has moved back a step away from the senses; you can't see or feel it anymore. It has moved back a step into the interior of the mind. It becomes much more abstract. We are at liberty to refuse this situation in our relations with phenomena. But abstraction becomes much more powerful than it might seem because with it one is more at the center of the way things work, one grasps more easily the way things generate themselves.

In physics, this was the case once it approached that degree of abstraction that grasps event at a statistical/mathematical level without the means to represent it mimetically. The result was an enormously increased power of controlling nature because one sees how it works, rather than just getting descriptive data. There is a similar movement in painting, obviously, from impressionism to cubism, in terms of *cultural* abstraction. Writing has been the slowest to move in that direction. There are two kinds of computers, the digital and the analog computer. The analog computer works basically according to imitation, it's a mimetic machine. In some way it reduces the data to analogous wavelengths and stores those wavelengths as information. Phenomena are represented in terms of models, basically. The digital computer abstracts the information in a form that has nothing to do with the phenomenon itself. The digital computer simply works on the base of a yes-no system. Each bit of data is just that yes-no distinction which finally amounts to some significant piece of information. It seems because of the simplicity of that process, more information can be stored more exactly. It is an odd paradox—the more abstract the computer process, the more concretely it can store and reproduce information. In that sense it seems to me that this process of abstraction began with Mallarmé. The curve that began with Mallarmé is still hanging in the air. It has certainly not been completed yet. You find it in Joyce and Beckett and to a certain extent in the nouveau roman and in some of the younger generation of writers in the States. They are groping for a language that can move us to another phase of abstraction that will allow that kind of power that the move into abstraction allowed in physics. That's a very hard battle because in fiction, everybody is still very much attached to the tradition of mimesis. It really is a very hard struggle and here Roussel is a great help.

When Roussel inhibits his own expressiveness in language to the extreme degree he does, he begins to deal with language speaking itself, something that you find also in Beckett in a different way, although we should not forget Gertrude Stein or Burroughs. Roussel begins to let language speak itself and that seems to me very important because language as the center of the culture, the generator of the culture, is a storehouse of knowledge, of information capable of random access, which is much greater than the individual's aptitude to make use of it for a particular purpose at a particular time. In that sense the whole idea of authorship changes. This is something that structuralist analysis deals with. The role of the author has become less important with the recognition that the language speaks the author. The traditional situation has become somehow inverted. The author operates a sort of a "mise en scene" which gives the language the opportunity to speak itself, the space to move.

From this point of view, you can say that individuals are nothing more than an extension of general language, rather than the other way around. For the humanist point of view, the individual, especially the genius, is the creator of the culture, but for this point of view it seems that it's the collective that is the important thing and the individual just happens to be in a more or less strategic position to allow the process to proceed at a more or less rapid rate. Roussel put his finger at the center of this process, getting away from the importance of the author to the importance of the medium. That's why I so much like the arbitrary. My version lately is to use arbitrary forms to deny my own expression in order to arrive at some release of the language and the culture through my work.

But there are big differences between European and American culture. In the "Paris-Paris" show there was a very interesting room with abstractions by Matthieu from 1945 to 1951. In the same room there was also a magnificent Pollock and a Sam Francis. My first thought was that Matthieu did certain things Pollock did, maybe before Pollock. I looked at the Pollock carefully. It was not the same thing at all. The difference between the paintings comes from the difference between American and European culture. In the Matthieu, there is still a sense of design, a sense of the frame and a sense of beauty even. In the Pollock it's completely flat with a minimal reference to the frame. The sense of form is, I would say without center—eccentric—there is an expression of energy that's very similar to what happens in jazz. The definition of the artifact becomes more a function of the act than a function of the traditional form. The beatniks, the Black Mountain writers, and the San Francisco writers picked up on both jazz and action painting. That sense of improvisation, fast invention, was one step in releasing language, in releasing language from both tradition and the individual ego. The language at this point certainly begins to speak itself instead of speaking for the author so much. The next phase I see in recent American fiction is the introduction of collage coming in through Gysin and Burroughs. It seems to be a European invention but in fact it had been perhaps the main technique for the revolution in modernist poetry earlier in the century. You can think of *The Waste Land* as a collage, the "Cantos," *Ulysses* is a collage, *Finnegans Wake* is one too. It was a way of pulling in a lot of new material, recombining it in a new form that created something unpremeditated, by juxtaposition. It's the ideal medium for an intellectual tourist like Ezra Pound.

Still more recently, Clarence Major does a combination of improvisation and the arbitrary, as in Roussel, sapping the prefabricated significance of his language. Major uses arbitrary techniques to do that. Somebody jumps off a bridge and then in the next paragraph he is still alive. The impossible and the arbitrary, the contradictory, reduce the significance of the language and fix it in a certain place which keeps it at the surface and does not allow it any traditional or associative profundity. That retains symbolic meaning but only in a process which is constantly throwing up new information. The symbols do not have static meaning. I think the idea of process has become important for some American writers. The idea that writing has got to do something instead of merely meaning something. Words carry so much meaning that we must be constantly fighting against the meaning of language in order to release other aspects of language that can be in fact more important. This is the point where Gertrude Stein is important because you can read Roussel as if it meant something though it does not. Gertrude Stein, when you are in front of certain of her texts, never allows you to do that.

Lavallé: You've been talking about the influence of jazz and action painting on writing. What about hyperrealism and rock, the two European phantasms about America. Did they have any influence on writing?

Sukenick: There is one way I and other writers worked with hyperrealism fifteen years ago when people spoke about the death of the novel. What was happening was that people had lost the sense that fiction represented anything important about the way they were living. One American answer to this was to invent a way of writing that brought more information, more data into a situation that had no meaning beyond data to begin with; it is not necessarily an auspicious strategy. In this case, the traditional Hemingway type novel had become so literary, so confined in its form that it could only allow us sentimental information. Various things began to break that down: faction, nonfiction novels, new journalism. Those writings were semifictive, semijournalistic (Tom Wolfe, Norman Mailer, Truman Capote). I took a different direction with the use of the tape recorder. That is a form of hyperrealism. I began doing imprints of reality with the tape recorder in 1969. I stopped doing it because I used a lot of improvisation with it and I got tired of improvisation. I'm going to use it again because I feel the need to introduce in my writing a lot of pure data and reduce the quotient of imagination. The important point is to be able to avoid mere reproduction of the data of the quotidian. The trick there is not to take it for granted that's what reality is—that is the problem with the nonfiction novel. Tom Wolfe talks about things that really happen and he says that James Joyce was trying to write what really happens in a journalistic sense. That's a little bit stupid to think that the journalistic version of something is any realer. If you find a way of integrating that data in an inventive way, it can become interesting. Here invention is parallel to that in photography—the important thing is what you choose to pay attention to.

There is something about the punk movement that is interesting and that is the idea of being ugly instead of being nice. It's like the comparison between the Pollock and the Matthieu. It breaks down the esthetic. If something looks beautiful when it is produced, forget it. It is only after the fact that a strong work becomes beautiful. When Pollock's work first came out I found it very savage. When I saw it a few days ago I thought it was very elegant and beautiful and the initially prettier Matthieu looked kind of cheap.

Charlotte Meyer: Characters in your novels seem to lose their identities all the time. What are your ideas about character?

Sukenick: I don't really believe in characterization in the old sense. A lot of my characterizations tend to take the form of a cartoon or sketch, or the characters tend to be very fluid. This represents my sense that character is much more heavily influenced from moment to moment by environment, both interior and exterior, than seemed to be the case in the traditional novel. In my fiction there is a heavier sense of the way situation can influence characterization in contemporary life. My books reflect this especially in the way the characters all tend to become part of a group mind; certainly a group mind seems to develop in *98.6* in the commune section, "The Children of Frankenstein." And I think it's true in contemporary life that the mind of the larger social unit, the *Zeitgeist*, is becoming more and more cohesive, whereas the sense of individual identity is becoming more and more diffuse. Part of the reason for that is the network of electronic communications that enables the social strata to act more and more the way a mind does, to process quickly large amounts of information for large numbers of people, and to focus it in one direction.

I also think the interior environment of the personality has become more fluid, more subject to immediate incident and circumstance than was true in the Victorian personality as portrayed in traditional fiction. The first sign you see of this change is when Lawrence reduces personality to a minimum germinal force beyond which all attributes are strictly incidental. My characters have some very basic minimal identity, but beyond that the changes they go through are enormous, even contradictory. I prefer the characters to be as little consistent with themselves as they can be, so that everything but that tiny, perhaps genetic, trace of identity is cancelled out. I haven't made a sociological or political estimate of the way contemporary polity is proceeding and then put that into my books. It's the other way around: I've discovered this through my books, and it seems to check out in the more objective social reality.

Meyer: Why are your novels always comic?

Sukenick: The ways that people react to the deepest experiences of their lives are physiologically limited: you react from the gut, or the diaphragm. So what kinds of reactions are possible from the diaphragm? Crying, laughing, vomiting. In writing, the parallels are tragedy, comedy, and maybe the grotesque. Maybe that's what the gothic is: you get so scared you puke. Violence or disgust—the grotesque.

Laughter is one way to release the tensions that are in fact reactions to the deepest things that confront us. Without laughter it's very hard to get into the really sad things. For example, one of the things I have against certain middlebrow writers who have big literary reputations is that they're very ponderous, very serious. I get deadened; I don't respond, even though they're talking about tragic situations. With writers like Céline, like Genet, who's funny in a certain way, Henry Miller, Rabelais, you can move into gut laughter, gut sadness. If one side is cut off, it is very rare that you can get the other side. Certainly Shakespeare had both sides . . . but Sophocles is not very funny.

But there's another thing about laughter—it's not a large form. You think of the overall form of a book: plot, narrative, character, beginning, middle, end. That's not funny. There's no way the form, the whole curve of a book, can be funny. And that's another reason why the forms of so many of the books I like (like Federman's and Katz's and so on) are loose curves of feeling, not very specific and hard. Books that are too formalized don't allow enough room for particulars, and particulars provoke laughter. The closest parallel to the stuff that we're doing is the work of the so-called black humorists of the sixties. The comics, especially Lenny Bruce in the sixties, were very influential on the black humorists; Philip Roth and Lenny Michaels particularly picked up a lot from him. That kind of style has had a great appeal for me. But fiction can do a lot more than that. I consider fiction the main reality-making art. And so I wanted to try to do other things with fiction.

Meyer: Your definition of the novel has changed from art-as-illusion to art-as-experience. How has the definition of the artist changed?

Sukenick: The artist becomes the inventor of experience from mere phenomena: that is, we're confronted with phenomena and we want experience. Experience is phenomena taken in and made relevant to the individual psyche.

Meyer: Do you consider yourself part of the Literature of Exhaustion?

Sukenick: The Literature of Exhaustion is based on the idea that modern fiction has become so self-conscious that it now is imitation of other forms. Partly I agree with that. We do live in media: not only in television and newspapers and so on, but in language and in images that are communicated and disseminated throughout the culture. What Barth is getting at is that writing is not holding a mirror up to nature but imitating culture forms. Writing is now imitation of other writing, which is an interesting idea and one that in many ways I agree with. But it's also a kind of dead end. There seems to be an intermediate step that Barth is leaving out, that is, contact with phenomena as they become experience. He believes that all you can and should do is exhaust the forms that have been created, and once you do, you presumably will arrive at new forms.

Meyer: One thing that seems to separate you from Barth is that all his forms are closed, that is, not improvised.

Sukenick: Right. When you imitate old forms you get those closed forms because you're stuck in literature, stuck in culture. The way I proceed is to push out to the edge of culture and of form and work always with open forms, which can in the language of some of the painters allow more reality into the work. I'm always working with collage and tape recorders, or the unpremeditated. I like forms which do not allow me to know what's going to happen next, even formally.

Meyer: Doesn't *Long Talking Bad Conditions Blues* have a closed form?

Sukenick: It has a closed form in terms of its linear and spatial structure, but the form is closed so that it can open to new material and generate new material that I would not have been able to think of without the form. The form of *Long Talking* is the fulfillment of a certain arithmetical structure which, however, is an empty structure, to be filled. Since it's an arbitrary form it carries no baggage with it, no implication of any particular content. It's like putting out a net. In some ways what you catch has to do with the dimensions and the shape of the net. I use a net with such and such space between the interstices and that means I'm going to catch flounder instead of trout.

Meyer: No water buffalo.

Sukenick: No water buffalo. No alligators. So in that sense the form is closed, but it's an enclosed emptiness which then has to be filled up in a certain way. That, it seems to me, is a way of getting back to the traditional notion of form, like the sonnet form, with the difference that the sonnet form carries too many implications of what should be there, whereas an arbitrary form is completely an open space, an empty space.

Meyer: When you talk about baggage carried with a form, do you mean that certain forms have usually dealt with certain subject matters, as, say, the sonnet is almost always about love or time?

Sukenick: Yes, not only subject matters but also certain tropes, certain kinds of rhetoric, certain moods and tones. It's hard, for example, to get away from the implications of blank verse once you've read the great blank verse writers in the English tradition. The rhythms and the syntax are already laid out and that dictates a certain range of content.

Meyer: Is that why you separate yourself from Barth, because he's limited in what he can talk about?

Sukenick: I'm not as self-conscious about culture as he is. I don't like to go through culture; I like to jump ahead and get to the edge of it, whereas he feels the need to take it into account. In a way it's a very Joycean ploy. *Finnegans Wake* has to incorporate everything so that, as the newest integration, it can transcend the whole culture. I'm like a fisherman with a fast boat that keeps pulling in fish and throwing them overboard. I like to travel light. I don't like texts that are burdened with the history of the whole culture. That's too modern for my tastes.

Meyer: Too modernist?

Sukenick: Too modernist. Modernism felt the need to recapitulate the whole culture and I feel that the whole culture has already been recapitulated and we now have the right— or the *Zeitgeist*, you might say, has earned the right—to move ahead.

Meyer: You seem to have thrown some very traditional fish overboard, like punctuation. Why is it that in your fiction punctuation does not mark out the syntax, the grammatical units? It's as if you're trying to capture instead the rhythm of vocalized language.

Sukenick: I use sentence rhythm in a variety of ways. Sometimes I use it against punctuation, using punctuation as a counterrhythm to get a fast, syncopated effect. Lately I've been writing in sentence fragments without punctuation at all, not imitating but actually entering into the rhythms of the body. Rhythm, I think, is a way of getting at information without circulating it through the conscious part of the brain.

Meyer: Is that what you were getting at in *98.6* with that prelapsarian creature, the Missing Lunk? The ideal connection between the body and the head?

Sukenick: Yes. Rhythm imparts a certain kind of information. The Greeks were aware of the meanings of various rhythms: one kind of music was martial, and so on. We still retain those concepts, but we don't elaborate them much. We have symphonic movements and the sonata form and rock and roll and punk rock and so on, but the possibilities for articulations and distinctions in kinds of rhythm are much greater than what we have now.

Meyer: What effect does arbitrary form have on composition? It forces you to certain heights of imagination?

Sukenick: Exactly. In the heroic couplet the need for constant rhyming and exact rhythm forces you to think of things you could not possibly otherwise have thought of. So there's an immediate interplay between the form and the improvisation. Improvising within that structure seems to me much more fun, much less slack, much more energetic, disciplined, and creative. I generate more surprises for myself all the time, more unforeseen twists and turns. But conventional forms carry too much baggage, so my current feeling is that it doesn't matter what the form is as long as it's a form. I don't want to write in sonnets. I think we need to go back to form, but not necessarily back to the Austro-Hungarian Empire. Or to the Elizabethan period.

Meyer: Numbers seem to be important to you. *Out* has 7 + 3 = 10 as a governing idea, for example, and you mentioned just now that *Long Talking* is based on the number seven. Why is that?

Sukenick: Numbers are arbitrary ways of organizing experience and I like arbitrary ways of organizing experience. The mind is something like the ocean to a reef, even an oil rig, or whatever kind of solid protrusion might occur in an oceanic environment. Because something happens to be where it is, for no particular reason, things begin to accrete to it. It doesn't matter too much where this arbitrary object is or how it's arranged or what it is, as long as it's there and the mind can begin its work on it. Perhaps there are some forms, some generative or formative ideas, that are better than others. And no doubt that has something to do with the biology of the brain and the history of a given time. But until we know more about those subjects, art in fact may be our best entree into them. That might be an interesting direction for criticism to take, the study of pure form. My own point of view is that form is strictly a means of release into your own experience, for a fuller recognition of your experience. And to get to the form that most successfully releases you into your experience, you may have to break through other forms that are preventing you from reaching it.

Meyer: Is it important for a writer of fiction to evolve a theoretical basis for what he or she is doing?

Sukenick: I don't think that's necessary at all. It's helpful to some writers to have theory; other writers hate theory. My feeling is that writing is itself a way of thinking and you don't need any abstract theory to interfere with that way of thinking. What is helpful is perhaps a rule-of-thumb theory, which is basically an extension of the writing and which feeds back into the writing and which also has the virtue of protecting you against various other ideologies or theories that get in the way of your writing or of its reception by others.

Jerzy Kutnik: What were your expectations after publishing *Up* and having it so well received? You must have been satisfied with the reception.

Sukenick: Yes and no. I was astounded by the reception and I had to do a lot of fancy footwork to regain my balance. When I grew up, I grew up with an idea of writing as a form of resistance to the establishment and culture at large. And I think that quality writers in the States have always, even if they haven't maintained that posture, started with that posture. Even the writers who went to Europe and turned out at the center of the establishment years later, like Hemingway, began as avant-gardists of sorts, as rebels. Hemingway was a rebel in the sense that writers in those days felt like they had to resist the culture, or get out of it. So they went to France. There was always some resistance on their part against the establishment which they considered hopeless in terms of its receptivity, its values, its cultivation. The point is that when I was growing up in the 50s and early 60s that was still the mentality. I still think it's the proper position for a writer in the States. That is, a writer is a critic of the society in my opinion. For a young writer who was beginning to write in, say, 1960, if he got published too quickly, he might himself think that he was doing something wrong, that if he could get accepted by the establishment that fast, he himself must be establishment, must be reflecting establishment values. So one was very cautious about that.

I expected my first novel to be totally rejected by the publishing industry. I expected that it would be published by some small press. Like the great modern texts which were always having that kind of problem, always being printed by nonindustry presses. And the big shock came for me when I gave it to a very powerful young literary agent, who immediately liked it and assured me that it could get published. I remember I was upset for two weeks after that. Then of course I thought, "Well, gee, maybe things have really changed, maybe the culture has really opened up." In fact, I think, it did really change at that point.

Kutnik: What was it that really changed? And what were the consequences?

Sukenick: There were two things that happened. One was that a lot of people then assumed that they could become rich and famous immediately, just like the Abstract Expressionists did, forgetting of course that Abstract Expressionists worked for twenty years in total obscurity. Then came Andy Warhol with his kind of avant-garde/establishment mentality and the merging of the avant-garde with the establishment that occurred partly through Warhol. And then you got Allen Ginsberg, who had been one of the Beat generation people— they had been fighting for years against the establishment and fighting a really difficult battle—in that picture, which was originally a poster for the *Evergreen Review* magazine, wearing a top hat, an Uncle Sam hat. It was posted all over the subways and everywhere. And it's interesting it was in the subways, because under the poster it said "Join the Underground." And everybody did, they all joined the underground. And it stopped being the underground. The whole situation changed, socially, of writers. You could no longer pretend to be a Dostoyevskian figure holed up in an attic or something of that sort creating great art. There were great artists who were not holed up but really on stage, on television. There was Norman Mailer's *Advertisements for Myself*, people pushing themselves in the media. The underground learned how to use the aboveground media. Artists got spoiled, much to the dismay of many young writers and painters and so on, who were given a lot of attention at first and then dropped like some commodity that had lost its vogue. And they had developed no interior logic of their own, they had adopted the logic of the market place. Because they had become so externalized, they had to simply depend on their market value as opposed to their own gyroscopes, artistic gyroscopes. That was the bad side—art and the mass market met and the mass market won, which could have been predicted.

The good part was that it was the end of modernism and the beginning of postmodernism, the end of an attitude which had become too precious with the moderns, and elitist, that the artist is separate from society and has to hole up and cannot have anything to do with the culture, can't try to affect it. It was now clear that, for better and for worse, the underground, the artist, the writer, could affect the culture in some way. A lot of artists started, instead of working as aliens outside the culture, working in and through the culture, trying to utilize the culture's institutions and methods. And if that didn't work—usually it didn't—they created shadow institutions, which is what we did with the Fiction Collective and the *American Book Review*. A whole alternate system.

Kutnik: The movement beyond the Western forms of thought was an important trend in the late 60s and the 70s, not only in fiction, but also in science, philosophy, social criticism, etc. Were you part of it?

Sukenick: Sure, why not? Although there was a lot about that trend that was merely trendy, and I hope I'm not being merely trendy. I'm just looking for ways to liberalize the role of the writer in the culture, because I find the options available to be too narrow. Some of the options that I can imagine or have heard about or read about seem much more rich. One possible model is that which Castaneda has created in his books. It is a situation in which you get the rationalistic man, who's taking his Ph.D., reverting to a more "primitive" culture through the mediation of the "primitive" medicine man he meets, who turns out to be very sophisticated and works off a tradition that's much richer than his own. So you get those conversations in which the rational man—Castaneda is Candide-like—is trying to explain what Don Juan is doing in rational language. And Don Juan keeps pulling him back into the world of the nonrational. I think something like that confrontation maybe was going on in fiction at that time. We were all looking for ways to find other roles for the writer.

Kutnik: Have your ideas concerning writing changed over the years? If so, what are the recent ones?

Sukenick: I have some ideas about not so much using my own language, of using the texts of society instead of my own language. I am trying to investigate the way language works in society. Or doing what the sculptor George Segal does. He just makes plaster casts of people. I find that very intriguing. In writing the equivalent of doing something like that would be tape recording. It strikes me that you can use a tape recorder to do that kind of thing.

Kutnik: What's the parallel?

Sukenick: The parallel is the idea of simply imprinting reality, getting an imprint of reality, or an imprint of phenomena. The tape would be like a plaster cast. Or another way I look at it is doing what I call "sonic snapshots," using the tape recorder like the camera. I'm at the point of deciding what my next movement in fiction is going to be. What I need to do now is, I think, to do everything I can to kill off the imaginary, the imaginative, anything that's made up, including the originality of language. I think that one of the unpleasant things that has happened in quality American writing is that it has suffered from a polarity between mass market popular writing and high art. Therefore, the books that are considered high art have sort of lost their root, their connection in the popular mind. To me a lot of books that the establishment accepts as being the opposite of mass market, the opposite of popular, are nothing but a thinned-out version of *belles-lettres*. One of the things I want to do is to really obliterate any of the possible cues that would cue a reader into thinking that I do that sort of thing. I want to intervene less in the writing. I'm not saying that I want to be less self-conscious. I want to move from the idea of the writer as creator to the idea of the writer as medium. I want things to work *through* me, to be the invisible intermediate step.

Kutnik: Do you mean to say that everybody can be a writer?

Sukenick: Everybody clearly can't be a medium. A medium is a quasi-religious personality. There are other ways of identifying what the writer should be than the way the Western bourgeois tradition labels the writer. For example, Ishmael Reed considers his writing in something like a tradition of voodoo, in which the writer is a kind of witch doctor and the books are spells. It's vastly different from the writer as the recorder or the super-reporter that he's supposed to be in Western tradition. And it's also a much more active role. I'm thinking of the writer as being the intermediary between the spiritual world, that is, the world of collective consciousness, and the world of the living. That's how I want to place myself as a writer.

Zoltán Abádi-Nagy: Jerome Klinkowitz wrote in *North American Review* in 1973 that you revitalize fiction "by having it do what it should: to make reality seem less unreal." What does the unreality of reality mean?

Sukenick: It means that phenomena have the feeling of being not meaningful in relation to the ego. How can I put it? It is like you are outside on a rainy day when you are tired and not feeling well and you feel very disconnected from the life around you and the phenomena around you. And on that occasion something may suddenly happen, the sun may come out or you might see a beautiful bird and suddenly the world comes alive and becomes reconnected with the ego.

Abádi-Nagy: So this is something pretty universal, not social primarily.

Sukenick: No. I think it is basically a fundamental psychological mechanism. Sometimes you feel connected with the life around you, and sometimes you feel very disconnected. It is like the way it is said that schizophrenics do not see colors sometimes. It seems to me the function of the imagination, one of its functions, is to vitalize the connection between self and phenomena.

Abádi-Nagy: What can the imagination do here, how can it make the unreal real?

Sukenick: It reconnects phenomena in some vital way with the needs of the ego, with the emotional needs of the ego.

Emotional in a large sense including a sense of purpose, identity, meaningfulness.

Abádi-Nagy: Reality becomes unreal and it is irrespective of a given historical time, it is psychological, as you say. Can it become unreal in any concrete social senses that you think the imagination has to deal with in a similar way?

Sukenick: I mean data is data. So the only thing there is to talk about is the way the mind will report it. I suppose there are historical periods that are so imposing in terms of their threat, or their chaos, that they begin to seem totally unreal. A good example is Auschwitz, that whole phenomenon of the liquidation of huge masses of people, especially when you talk about a place where so much of it was done. It is very hard to grasp, very hard to connect in any way with one's own ego. And in a certain sense there may be some wisdom, some unconscious wisdom in that because it may be that too great an influx of unconditioned data at certain points may be maddening. This kind of thing, I suppose, happened to people who took LSD and lost control of the censorship of the senses and the intelligence so that undifferentiated data flooded the mind.

Abádi-Nagy: Your idea is somewhat different from what is considered the traditional function of art where art would be expected to call the reader's attention to such unreal aspects of reality. You want to reconnect the reader in some other way.

Sukenick: If you are talking about, for example, the idea of defamiliarization . . .

Abádi-Nagy: Yes . . .

Sukenick: I think defamiliarization actually increases the reality quotient of phenomena. Because what happens is you get used to seeing something, let us say seeing something in a particular formulated way and it begins to lose any kind of important identity for you so that when it is defamiliarized you look at it more sharply and realize what it is again. I feel that I have a real attachment to the data of our lives as opposed to, say, the French school of criticism, which—I have had this argument with Federman—concentrates more on language and the self-enclosed quality of language as opposed to its connection with reality. For me the whole purpose of the imagination in writing is to constantly destroy the formulations of language, to make language work against itself so that there can be an openness to data. Or you might say that I see it as a cyclical thing. A metaphor for reality is created but then in order to see reality again you have to destroy the metaphor and see the source of the metaphor. But I really do think that the point of rhetoric is to constantly try to connect with phenomena rather than to get caught up in figurations.

Abádi-Nagy: Why do you call attention to the text in your fiction?

Sukenick: I will put it this way. What I am trying to do is call attention to the text itself so that it becomes not a window which seems to look out onto the world but a kind of object that returns the reader to his own imagination. I am trying to cut this circuit that mimesis creates in which the work gives the illusion of being a picture of the world. I am trying to make the work something that reminds the reader of how he himself thinks and what he is thinking, and thereby trying to activate his imagination so that he himself can look at the world, not necessarily in my version of it—in his own version of it. That is the point of always calling attention to the text in my work. It is not a kind of narcissistic phase of consciousness. On the contrary, it is a way of trying to make the reader conscious of his own mind, the functioning of his own imagination as the writer is aware of the functioning of the text. So that the imagination is then activated, ready to go back to reality in some revitalized way. In a certain sense it is like a Brechtian idea: to try to stop that process of mimesis and catharsis, which I feel is escapist. Instead I am trying to return the reader to himself and his world, but revitalized.

Abádi-Nagy: How does fiction that rejects the mimetic model help us work out the essentials of our fate?

Sukenick: Because once you drop the pretense that the novel is giving an image of reality you can then begin to think about such issues as what reality is after all, how we can use our imaginations on it, what it is that controls the idea of reality. I think once you begin to talk about that stuff, once you call it into question, it becomes immediately obvious that we are not talking about reality at all but authority, that it is a question of who and what has the power to make authoritative statements about phenomena. Then, I think, we are dealing with our fate in a much more direct way, we are talking about who controls our imaginations or what controls our imaginations, what has the authority to do so, whether it is proper authority, whether we want it to control our imaginations. Maybe something other than what we want to control our imaginations is controlling them. Then we can really begin to talk about the way our lives go from day to day, whether it is being just, for example, manipulated by politics, the media or the mass market in the United States. There is a slogan that I use for students when I am trying to get them on to the subject, in other words, I am trying to get them into this way of thinking: "If you don't use your own imagination, somebody else is going to use it for you."

Abádi-Nagy: Are you concerned with the idea that art begins with a wound which the artist attempts to heal?

Sukenick: Well, I have nothing against the "wound and the bow" idea of artistic composition and I think that may well be true for me or for any writer at the level of personal therapy, but for me there are other things that are much more important. It seems to me that art in its own right can stand beside other investigations into the nature of what we call reality, and stand beside them without therapeutic excuse. That is, only if you can think of, let us say, the investigation of history as therapy, which maybe it is in some way, or, let us say, the investigation of the nucleus of the atom as therapy, only then would I admit that art is basically therapeutic. To me art is simply a way of thinking which can be used for many things. It can be used for therapy but it can also be used for all sorts of investigations that are much more positive than therapy.

Abádi-Nagy: Does improvisation lend an inner structure to the work?

Sukenick: Yes. The key to successful improvisation is that structure develops and that structure is unforeseen. I think if structure does not develop in improvisation then the improvisation is no good. But the thing is that it is totally unpremeditated structure, it is structure that you have to do while you are on your toes performing. I mean a great example is a jazz solo. If you examine a Charlie Parker solo that was improvised, I am absolutely certain you will find a very intense, intricate structure. But the structure will be probably more on the micro than the macro level, more in the details than the overall form because it goes from moment to moment, so the process of improvisatory composition almost requires that you are structuring at a very minute level, a very small unit of composition rather than at the level of the larger units of composition. But structure I am sure it will be, it can be a question of assonance, a question of repetition of ideas, but something develops. In fact, to tell you the truth, I think what improvisation really depends on is the fact that the mind wants release from larger structures. It simply cannot be unstructured. I find it is almost impossible to write nonsense unless I try very hard and use some arbitrary means to do it. Our minds are very organized and what you are doing when you are improvising is removing the larger structures as you are releasing other structures, structures you did not know were there and therefore structures that are real discoveries and can be very useful.

Abádi-Nagy: You would agree that your kind of fiction is not available to a mass audience? That if any average reader—in an awareness of a little theory that is needed to understand what is going on—would wish to understand and appreciate your work, he will not find it possible?

Sukenick: I think that is not the real question. If my work is not available to a mass market audience, it is not available in more ways than one. First of all, they could not get it if they wanted it, and second of all, they would not have the training or the critical bridge necessary. It seems to me that in catering to the mass market and popular forms Gerald Graff is prostituting himself to the system. These kinds of critics typically have the idea that radical content in conventional form is going to have some kind of radicalizing effect. I think that is nonsense. I think that is a way of co-opting the writer. It seems to me the only way that you are going to make a dent is to do something like the Beat Generation did: have a new kind of content in a new kind of form, and the formal element is very important because otherwise people just go on thinking the same way they always thought but with a slight refocusing. You try as best you can to make that new form something that is available to people. And that is not necessarily something that is within one's control; some people will become popular, some people won't.

Abádi-Nagy: Let us say that experience, which is chaotic all right, but not all chaos, occasionally organizes itself into some pattern, it suggests some logic, some causation. Would you say that you programmatically refuse to explore that?

Sukenick: You mean, when experience itself is self-organizing?

Abádi-Nagy: Yes.

Sukenick: No, not at all, There are times, when, for example, I use the tape recorder to record an experience. Sometimes experience has in itself the quality of a story, itself the quality of a complete unit. If that is the case, then the element of imagination can be almost zero whereas in other cases where things are more chaotic, the element of the imagination needs to be more active, needs to add more. So sometimes imagination is a function that depends on the way things are going. It does not always have the exact same function. Sometimes you need it a lot, sometimes you need it less, and when experience seems to be self-organizing—for example, on a beautiful sunny day when you are happy and everything seems to be just right—it is as if the world's imagination were working, and yours is not necessary.

Abádi-Nagy: In *Lost in the Funhouse*, John Barth concludes that the old analogy between novel and world can no longer be employed and one thing that follows is that "fiction must acknowledge its fictitiousness and metaphoric invalidity." I find that very close to your idea that fiction is nothing but fiction.

Sukenick: But there is a gap and I think it is typical between these creative generations. There is a step he does not take. He says that fiction must acknowledge its fictitiousness. I would agree with this. Then he says "and the invalidity of its metaphors." There I do not agree. I think that the metaphors *are* valid. Fictitiousness is never legitimate on the level he thinks it ought to have been, the way it seemed to be in the nineteenth century. That is, those images of reality are always metaphors like kleenex that are to be used and to be thrown away and then there is the next metaphor ahead, in other words, they have an impermanent validity, it seems to me. Or you might say that fiction is valid without metaphor. Kleenex is not a metaphor, that's why it's useful.

Joe David Bellamy: How do you feel about the characters in your fiction?

Sukenick: I feel they're sort of dialectical divisions of my own personality, this trend and that trend. But that's only half of it. The other half of it is that, in any case, I feel that the imagination is a faculty of perception. It's not an extra faculty, but a faculty that's essential, that one uses all the time. Otherwise you couldn't get along from one moment to the next. I mean, you're always making people up, in effect. I mean, like, there you are, and I don't know much about you; but, in a way, I'm making you up. I'm filling up the gaps in my mind, and I create the person who happens to be there. And probably there's a great gap between my version and yours. Genet, clearly, as he comes through in his books, is an artifice—and sheer artifice. First of all, there's the sense in which a homosexual has made up his own character anyway because it involves a denial of masculinity—for some homosexuals. It seems to for Genet. That particular type of homosexual is then proceeding on the basis of artifice, very clearly. Now I think one reason why Genet is important is that in his case it's an extreme transition. It simply makes clear what we all do, you see what I mean? It's especially clear in the case of a transvestite homosexual, a queen. I think that, in fact, we have a certain amount of data about ourselves that we know about, and we organize it in this way or that way according to this or that ego structure. And then, in fact, people's sense of themselves shifts according to situations that they find themselves in, and even more drastically according to traumatic experiences they might pass through in their lives.

I think this is reflected in a whole literary trend. I don't think the kind of books I'm interested in are interested in characterization anymore. In Kafka you get K. In *Finnegans Wake* you get characters who are totally fluid. One person becomes another person. H. C. E. becomes Persse O'Reilly or this or that. People are constantly changing persona within a limited range. There's the father figure or the king figure, and anything that fits into that is H. C. E., and it keeps changing. And it's not only a personality change, it's a time change. With Joyce and with Kafka you get a cipher; you don't get a character. You get K., who is a character but in a linguistic sense. And in Beckett you sometimes get somebody who's a locus who not only doesn't know who he is, he doesn't know what he is—I guess that's the extreme—and in Henry Miller you get the whole process. You get somebody who is consciously trying to destroy his own character.

Bellamy: What are taboo subjects now?

Sukenick: I think it's actually very hard to escape personal taboos, because it's very hard to escape personal repression. And I suddenly, at one point, had the overwhelming realization that I was just—you know. . . . Well, the way it happened was this: I did a double-take—because I started thinking of writing something, and then I had a reaction that was almost subconscious which went: I can't write that. But for some reason it was just conscious enough for me to catch it, and I suddenly realized the extent to which I was censoring myself. What happened was I caught myself just on the verge of forgetting the whole episode. It went like this: idea to write something, I can't write that, forget it! And in another second it would have been obliterated. For some reason, I caught it and realized the degree that I was cancelling things out. That was a very important moment for me, crucial maybe.

Bellamy: I'm not trying to diminish the importance of a work as a literary or esthetic achievement, say. I'm just trying to get at some of the possible psychological reasons why fiction exists.

Sukenick: I think there are epistemological reasons before there are psychological reasons. After all, myth is a way of organizing the world that antecedes philosophy.

Bellamy: Okay. I agree. That gets through everything, it seems to me.

Sukenick: I mean, my whole idea about fiction is that it's a normal, if I may use the word, epistemological procedure; that is, it is at the very center of everybody all the time at any period; and you don't have to search for psychological reasons, although they may be there too. But I think the epistemological ones are far more important and anterior. It's a way of making up the world and making sense of it.

Bellamy: I was interested in what you were saying about Henry Miller. You were discussing his personality as a major aspect of his works and of the characters in his books. That is, you emphasized that his character is predominant. And you called it a manifestation of an exemplary personality. And also, you talked about the tendency of his works to be—outside the novel or to get away from art. I was wondering why you seem to think *that* is what he is doing. And, also, I thought of your own books, which seem to be involved in a related sort of activity. Why is that not like a novel? Or why is it not art at least?

Sukenick: Well, of course, I do believe it's art. It's not like the standard idea of art, that's all. It's not art with a capital

"A." It's not *kulchur*. It's art, of course. It just breaks out of a formula of what art ordinarily is conceived to be, what the novel is ordinarily conceived to be.

Bellamy: Do you think of the novel as a set form—as this kind of thing that's already happened in history, and not as a thing that's progressing and changing all the time?

Sukenick: Well, I think that the kind of imaginative act that goes into a novel, let's say fiction, is so basic to human consciousness that, you know, it antedates the novel, and the novel is a particular form of it.

I don't really think that novels should come out of a tradition of the novel. I think they should come out of your own experience—especially now when our present seems very discontinuous from a recent past. It seems to be all the more important that you should get rid of old forms and allow new forms to grow out of your own experience. It seems to me that the novel form is a block, that there are all these talented people around trying to write in this form which doesn't suit them at all; so that instead of releasing their energies, it blocks them out.

James Nagle: Where do you see the current trend going in about fifteen years?

Sukenick: I don't think I've thought that far ahead. I think it's unpredictable. I think it depends on a lot of cultural and sociological variables, which enter into the work, which I can't pretend to know about. I also think that it's dangerous to try to think about art as a historical progression with movements succeeding one another because then you are always looking for the next wave and its rationale. And finally the rationale, the criticism, becomes more important than the work. So I prefer to make statements that are dispensable, that you can throw away. And the kind of suggestions I make in these digressions are like that. I hesitate to make any kind of prediction because in a way the very idea is that fiction is unpredictable as well as undefinable, except by itself.

Nagle: Doesn't that imply that writers themselves would make the best critics?

Sukenick: There was a time, I have heard, at Harvard, when they were thinking of hiring Nabokov, and somebody said, "Well, you don't need the elephant in the zoology class." But I would like to insist that there is a kind of writer's criticism that is extremely important and there are kinds of that criticism that straddle both academic and nonacademic realms, Eliot's for example. I would say that that kind of contemporary criticism is largely unknown in the academic area. It's very important to writers, and at its best moments consistently produces the best criticism on any terms. I would also like to argue that writers are becoming more conscious of what they are doing and more able to tell you what they are doing. I know that many writers still don't like to talk about what they are doing because they feel it spoils the mystery. But I suspect that may be a pose which perpetuates facile mysteries. There will always be a mystery, of course. But I do think that fiction writers and poets are capable of making their own case on an equal basis with academic criticism.

III. Wallace Stevens: Theory and Practice

Abbreviations

CP	*The Collected Poems of Wallace Stevens.* New York: Alfred A. Knopf, 1954.
LWS	*Letters of Wallace Stevens,* edited by Holly Stevens. New York: Alfred A. Knopf, 1966.
NA	*The Necessary Angel.* New York: Alfred A. Knopf, 1951.
OP	*Opus Posthumous,* edited by Samuel French Morse. New York: Alfred A. Knopf, 1957.
MD	*Mattino Domenicale ed Altre Poesie,* translated by Renato Poggioli. Torino: Giulio Einaudi, 1954.

The Reality of the Imagination

Excessive attention to Wallace Stevens's theory can obscure what his poetry is about. His subject might best be described at the outset, for the sake of simplicity, in terms of the question posed in the early poem, "The American Sublime": "How does one stand/To behold the sublime/ . . . how does one feel?" (*CP*, pp. 130–31). This is less an ideological question than it is one of stance or posture: With what tenable attitude may one confront the difficult circumstances of contemporary American secular life and avail oneself of the good possible in it? How, in short, does one get along? Writing poetry was for Stevens a way of getting along. He must be taken seriously when he says that he writes poetry because he needs to (*OP*, p. xxxvii). The act of composition was for him a way of discovering and crystallizing what he called in one of his last poems, "Local Objects," "the objects of insight, the integrations/Of feeling . . ."

That were the moments of the classic, the beautiful.
These were that serene he had always been approaching.
   (*OP*, p. 112)

These are discoveries not of the good, but simply of good things "As when the sun comes rising, when the sea/Clears deeply" (*CP*, p. 398), times "when the cock crows on the left and all/Is well" (*CP*, p. 386)—whose revelation composes the poet in the composition of his poem.

This composure in face of what Stevens calls "the pressure of reality," this "serene" which is, at its extreme, a highly intense state of mind, stands as a kind of ideal experience which is central to Stevens's poetry. His theories, the heroes and fictions he hypothesizes, are tentative efforts to recapture and formularize it so that the experience may cease to be merely fortuitous. Through it he seeks to achieve a rapport with the conditions of contemporary life within the limits of what that life will allow him to believe, within what is credible. He does not merely evade or condemn what he considers the spiritual and imaginative impoverishment of contemporary reality, but takes it as given and makes of it what he can. Frank Kermode has aptly said of Stevens, in contrast with his "great contemporaries": "In an age of poetic myth-making Stevens is almost alone in his respect for those facts which seem 'in disconnexion, dead and spiritless.' "[1] It is in his willingness to accept the fact of contemporary life that Stevens, as Irving Howe has put it, has begun to move beyond the "crisis of belief" that troubled his contemporaries, to the question, "how shall we live with and perhaps beyond it?"[2]

The desire for faith does not issue for Stevens, as it does for some of his contemporaries, in an attempt to utilize or rehabilitate older belief. The orientation of his poetry is historical, but this awareness of history works toward freeing it from the past for a more acute perception of the present. Myth, once recognized as such, is regarded as at best a noble falsification of the present based on the assumptions of the past or, in other words, as quixotic. The "final belief" in a "fiction" proposed in "Asides on the Oboe" (CP, p. 250) is discovered by the end of the poem to be nothing less than a full recognition of our humanity, divorced from such falsification. Stevens's poetry expresses what might be called a nostalgia for perfection, or an idea of perfection, which sometimes gives his thought a Platonic tone, but, like his nostalgia for our religious myth, this is merely nostalgia. Stevens recognizes an innate obsolescence in myth as crystallized perception of reality, and addresses himself therefore to immediate perception of the changing present as the most likely way to discover what we can or do in fact believe. (Although Stevens thought poetry could articulate the "credible," that which it is possible to believe, he did not claim that the function of poetry is the creation of systematic belief: "Poetry does not address itself to beliefs. Nor could it ever invent an ancient world full of figures that had been known and become endeared to its readers for centuries" [*NA*, p. 144.]) Adequate adjustment to the present can only be achieved through ever fresh perception of it, and this is the effort of his poetry. It tries to find what is fresh and attractive in a reality that is frequently stale and dispiriting by way of coming to a satisfactory rapport with it.

In order to arrive at such a rapport it is necessary to satisfy the extrarational but nonetheless real need for positive belief within the conditions of an indifferent and changing reality, as, for example, the desire to maintain a noble conception of human life. It is the constant irrational force of this desire that Stevens has in mind when he speaks of nobility as "a violence from within that protects us from a violence without" (*NA*, p. 36). But though the need for belief is not rational, it may be rationally understood, as Freudian psychology makes the irrational mechanics of desire available to the understanding and control of the reason. Thus, referring to Freud, Stevens suggests the possibility of a "science of illusions" (*NA*, p. 139). If one thinks of illusion as that created by the painter as he discovers the beauty of a landscape in his composition, or as that comprised in the poet's rhetorical formulations about reality, it is roughly equivalent to Stevens's idea of a "fiction" in which he resolves the problem of belief. A fiction is not an ideological formulation of belief but a statement of favorable rapport with reality sufficiently convincing that disbelief may be suspended. Stevens defines poetic truth as "an agreement with reality" believed, for a time, to be true (*NA*, p. 54). The "truth" of a fiction is poetic truth.

Because the fiction mediates between the requirements of desire and the conditions of reality, and because the relation between the two keeps changing, no statement of that relation is final. On the contrary, such statements do and must become constantly outmoded. It is like a game which, lacking any purpose but the playing of it, can only be played again and again. The urbane playfulness of Stevens's wit suggests his consciousness of this. His sense of humor is a way of expressing thought's perspective on its own limitations, its awareness that it must be ultimately outwitted by the extrarational forces between which it mediates.

Change

Stevens's poetry deals in a series of antithetic terms, such as chaos and order, imagination and reality, stasis and change. The repeated recombination of the terms in each antithesis produces a continual restatement of the shifting relation between them:

Two things of opposite natures seem to depend
On one another, as a man depends
On a woman, day on night, the imagined
On the real. This is the origin of change.
    (*CP*, p. 392)

In considering such antithetic terms Stevens will adopt the point of view of one, then of the other, and then that of some nuance between the two. He was a poet who, in this sense, refused to make up his mind because he believed that change was the life of the mind: "It can never be satisfied, the mind, never" (*CP*, p. 247; compare "An Ordinary Evening in New Haven," X, *CP*, p. 472). William York Tindall has written that Stevens usually brings conflicts to an end "by an agreement of opposites; for he had looked into Hegel."[3] I do not believe that Stevens was dialectical in this sense, for his syntheses are momentary, unstable, and, instead of advancing his argument, always break down into the original antithetic terms. That is why the relation between such terms must be continually restated, and it accounts for that constant reformulation of a cluster of ideas that comprises so much of Stevens's poetry. The first stanza of "An Ordinary Evening in New Haven" describes the procedure of the poem: a statement about the nature of reality followed by progressive qualification.

The eye's plain version of a thing apart,
The vulgate of experience. Of this,
A few words, an and yet, and yet, and yet—
    (*CP*, p. 465)

The rest of the poem consists of an exploration of the relations possible between the plain view of reality and its opposite, the imaginative view.

It is only another manifestation of this antithetic character that despite his acknowledgement of change, Stevens longed for peace, for stasis, for an unchanging ideal: "He wanted his heart to stop beating and his mind to rest/In a permanent realization" (*CP*, p. 425). Stevens's poetry gropes toward a final formulation that does not exist, one such as might be given by the tantalizing "impossible possible philosophers' man" who sums us up (*CP*, p. 250), and hence no single formulation can remain satisfactory. The "philosophers' man" is a fiction which must change as the exigencies which made it necessary change. One might reach beyond the quotidian to some finality, but, as Stevens put it in the early "The Man Whose Pharynx Was Bad" (*CP*, p. 96), "time will not relent."

In Stevens's conception, history is a process in which no idea of reality is final, poetry is a progressive metamorphosis of reality, and reality itself is an entity whose chief characteristic is flux. Man

Lives in a fluid, not on solid rock.
The solid was an age, a period
With appropriate, largely English, furniture . . .
Policed by the hope of Christmas.
    (*OP*, p. 68)

Verrocchio's statue of Colleoni represents for Stevens the static ideal left behind by dynamic history. The idea of nobility it embodies is no longer appropriate to the changed conditions for nobility in a new historical situation. As a symbol for belief it has failed to withstand the pressure of a new reality and has consequently become incredible: "It seems, nowadays, what it may very well not have seemed a few years ago, a little overpowering, a little magnificent" (*NA*, p. 9). Failing as a symbol of belief, the statue has become a magnificent artifact. Artifacts also are the statues in "Dance of the Macabre Mice" (*CP*, p. 123), in "Lions in Sweden" (*CP*, p. 124), and in the first two parts of "Owl's Clover," where the sculpted group of horses loses meaning in face of the bitter old woman: "The mass of stone collapsed to marble hulk" (*OP*, p. 44). The statue seemed "a thing from Schwarz's" (*OP*, p. 47)—the reference is most likely to F.A.O. Schwarz, the well known toy store—hence, a toy, a plaything, not to be taken seriously. So also, the "great statue of the General Du Puy" (in "Notes toward a Supreme Fiction") belonged "Among our more vestigial states of mind" (*CP*, pp. 391–92).

But although no faith is absolute, particular beliefs are credible for particular epochs. Stevens writes out of a situation in which the beliefs that once ordered reality have become incredible; but the soul "still hankers after sovereign images" (*CP*, p. 124). Stevens is concerned with discovering belief that is credible in the American present. The style by which Claude Lorraine achieved serenity is obsolete (*CP*, p. 135), "Marx has ruined Nature" (*CP*, p. 134)—by replacing it as a source of salvation, for such as Wordsworth, with the means of production and distribution or, more simply, with history—and "The heaven of Europe is empty, like a Schloss/ Abandoned because of taxes" (*OP*, p. 53). "The epic of disbelief/Blares oftener and soon, will soon be constant" (*CP*, p. 122). It is the function of poetry to meet this situation: "It has to face the men of the time and to meet/The women of the time" (*CP*, p. 240).

In a world whose fundamental condition is change, the only tenable kind of belief must involve an affirmation of change. There is no value in history beyond the content of the present as it comes and passes. In "Owl's Clover" this condition is figured in a "trash can" of beliefs where fragments of the statue are found:

There lies the head of the sculptor in which the thought
Of lizards, in its eye, is more acute
Than the thought that once was native to the skull;
And there are the white-maned horses' heads . . .
Parts of the immense detritus of a world
That is completely waste, that moves from waste
To waste, out of the hopeless waste of the past
Into a hopeful waste to come.
    (*OP*, p. 49)

"Nothing is final," chants the sun like Walt Whitman singing, "No man shall see the end" (*CP*, p. 150), and therefore, once more in the words of "Owl's Clover," "It is only enough/To live incessantly in change" (*OP*, p. 50).

Stevens's theory comprises more of a mechanics, or psychology, of belief than an assertion of particular belief. His fundamental assumption is that belief is a psychological process through which it is possible to arrive at an affirmative relation to one's environment. Like other needs, the need for an affirmative relation to reality, the "passion for yes" (*CP*, p. 320), has a repetitive pattern of desire, fulfillment, and ennui in a cycle that generates its own perpetuation. No part of the pattern is absolutely bad because all the parts are essential to the continuity of the cycle. Thus in "No Possum, No Sop, No Taters," when the crow who is part of the sterility and temporary stasis of the winter landscape rises up, "One joins him there for company,/But at a distance, in another tree" (*CP*, p. 294). The condition of the landscape is not a good to embrace but an evil to be tolerated as part of the ultimately benign cycle of change. This is "The last purity of the knowledge of good" to which the poem refers. Nor, correspondingly, is fulfillment itself absolutely good, as in "Banal Sojourn" (*CP*, p. 62), where the fulfillment of summer is described as having become a surfeit. This pattern is repeated in the cycle of the seasons as they affect the emotions, with winter representing barrenness; spring, desire; summer, fulfillment; and autumn, the decay of desire, a kind of asceticism.[4] The beginning of each emotional season is an experience of freshness and the end one of ennui and impatience for change (the onset of winter is sometimes an exception, an occasion for gloom). The vital point is that nothing should impede the continuity of the process on which the stimulation of desire and its satisfaction depend.

Because of this affirmation of change, the traditional lament of transitoriness is transformed in Stevens's poetry to a hymn of praise. Change is not less destructive, but this destruction is desirable and the imagination must help to execute it:

The mind is the great poem of winter, the man,
Who, to find what will suffice,
Destroys romantic tenements
Of rose and ice.
(*CP*, p. 238)

The mind reduces belief to the wintery barrenness of disbelief. But what it destroys is belief that is inadequate, and in so doing purges the world of

. . . an old delusion, an old affair with the sun,
An impossible aberration with the moon,
A grossness of peace.
(*CP*, p. 239)

A new resolution in the credible must follow one that is no longer satisfactory, as the satisfactions of one season are replaced by another season with satisfactions of its own:

The spring will have a health of its own, with none
Of autumn's halloo in its hair. So that closely, then,
Health follows after health. Salvation there:
There's no such thing as life; or if there is,
It is faster than the weather, faster than
Any character. It is more than any scene.
(*CP*, p. 192)

There is no one relation to, or agreement with, reality that can be called "life," and the many possible relations succeed one another as they are appropriate. To live in the health of change, therefore, is to live always in a present of constant change. Time is

. . . apart from any past, apart
From any future, the ever-living and being,
The ever-breathing and moving, the constant fire.
    (*CP*, p. 238)

The celebration of time, as in the literal march of time of
"Dutch Graves in Bucks County," is directed to time as it represents an ongoing break from history that frees the mind to
live in an agreement with the present: "And you, my sembla-
bles, in gaffer-green,/Know that the past is not part of the
present" (*CP*, p. 291). This is the benevolence of time, that
comes with its destructive power: "Freedom is like a man
who kills himself/Each night, an incessant butcher" (*CP*, p.
292). But despite time's purgative function in creating "An
end of evil in a profounder logic" (*CP*, p. 291), its destruc-
tiveness remains:

Men came as the sun comes, early children
And late wanderers creeping under the barb of night,
Year, year and year, defeated at last and lost
In an ignorance of sleep with nothing won.
    (*CP*, p. 291)

Within these terms of evil, the good finds its limits:

. . . The assassin discloses himself,
The force that destroys us is disclosed, within
This maximum, an adventure to be endured
With the politest helplessness.
    (*CP*, p. 324)

Chaos and Order

The perception of chaos comes for Stevens when reality
seems void of meaning and without emotional connection

with the ego. It is suggested by the sea as in "The Comedian as the Letter C"; by the barrenness of winter as in the "Nothing that is not there and the nothing that is" of "The Snow Man"; by the "large" (vastness, or infinitude) as in "the last largeness" of "The Curtains in the House of the Metaphysician"; by darkness as in "Domination of Black"; by "the blank" as in "Notes toward a Supreme Fiction" (CP, p. 397), or by "this blank cold" of "The Plain Sense of Things"; by the decay of autumn that reveals the bare essentials of the landscape, or by a decaying culture whose order no longer seems credible. Chaos is reality apprehended without the projections of the ego, so that we find ourselves in the position of "intelligent men/At the centre of the unintelligible" (CP, p. 495),[5] and thus alienated from the reality of which we are part.

But this indifferent, unintelligible chaos of reality without the imagination, which is what Stevens calls "absolute fact," is also that solid world beyond rhetoric and the imagination in which the ego may uniquely find fulfillment of desire. Thus Stevens qualifies his description of absolute fact as "destitute of any imaginative aspect whatever," by adding: "Unhappily the more destitute it becomes the more it begins to be precious" (NA, p. 60). The indifferent reality beyond the ego is the data with which the imagination works, the rock, as "The Man with the Blue Guitar" puts it (CP, p. 179), "To which his imagination returned,/From which it sped." Moreover, when one comes to accept this chaos as the only truth in the sense that it is the only order that exists, it may be brought into gratifying relation with the ego:

. . . having just
Escaped from the truth, the morning is color and mist,
Which is enough.
        (CP, p. 204)

One may then enjoy a pleasurable relation with reality in which the ego demands from the chaos of reality nothing but what it can give, and chaos is therefore adequate to satisfy the desires of the ego. In this state one simply enjoys the sense of one's own existence in a physical reality, beyond any meaning of that existence imposed by the ego: "It was how the sun came shining into his room:/To be without a description of to be" (*CP*, p. 205). Thus, the formulations of "Connoisseur of Chaos" (*CP*, p. 215): "A violent order is disorder" because it is imposed on, and therefore falsifies, the chaos of reality; and "A great disorder is an order" because, although "The squirming facts exceed the squamous mind," although reality proves incomprehensible to the ego, yet beyond the comprehending mind, a sense in this disorder is felt:

. . . yet relation appears,
A small relation expanding like the shade
Of a cloud on sand, a shape on the side of a hill.

In the terms of "The Man with the Blue Guitar" (*CP*, p. 169), the chaos of the storm is brought to bear, is brought into significant relation with the ego. The ego imposes no order on reality, therefore "the structure/Of things" is accepted "as the structure of ideas" (*CP*, p. 327). Reality is recognized as the unique source of the ego's content, thereby bridging "the dumbfoundering abyss/Between us and the object" (*CP*, p. 437) that alienates us from it, and allowing the ego to find fulfillment in reality.[6]

It is his poetry that gets Stevens from reality as chaos to reality as perceived in some kind of order by the ego. This may be seen in his use of images:

When the blackbird flew out of sight,
It marked the edge
Of one of many circles.
    (*CP*, p. 94)

This, from "Thirteen Ways of Looking at a Blackbird,"
demonstrates the way an image may be used as a principle of
order. The blackbird, seen as a point of reference, defines an
intelligible area among many possible but undefined intelligible areas. Speaking of "resemblances," the name Stevens
gives to the basis of metaphor, comparison, he says: "What
the eye beholds may be the text of life. It is, nevertheless, a
text that we do not write. The eye does not beget in resemblance. It sees. But the mind begets in resemblance as the
painter begets in representation; that is to say, as the painter
makes his world within a world" (*NA*, p. 76). The mind orders reality not by imposing ideas on it but by discovering
significant relations within it, as the artist abstracts and composes the elements of reality in significant integrations that
are works of art.

    It can be seen from this description of chaos and order that,
as he presents no particular belief, Stevens presents no particular order but a theory of order, just as one might teach a
theory of painting without advocating one style over another.
He affirms the chaos of reality and seeks through the imagination for ways to make it tolerable, and even a positive
good. This affirmation of chaos may not, in theory, seem an
effective means to order, but when one comes upon it in
"Sunday Morning" the case is different: "We live in an old
chaos of the sun" (*CP*, p. 70). So stated, chaos seems good
and the world seems ennobled by its identification with chaos. This is not a "truth" assumed for its usefulness even

though it is untrue. It is a way of thinking about something, a way of thinking about something that promotes a way of feeling about something. Again, the evocation of an unintelligible cosmos is not ordinarily sympathetic. This is "The Curtains in the House of the Metaphysician" (*CP*, p. 62):

It comes about that the drifting of these curtains
Is full of long motions; as the ponderous
Deflations of distance; or as clouds
Inseparable from their afternoons;
Or the changing of light, the dropping
Of the silence, wide sleep and solitude
Of night, in which all motion
Is beyond us, as the firmament,
Up-rising and down-falling, bares
The last largeness, bold to see.

This says nothing true or untrue about the chaos of reality in terms of absolute fact, but merely presents a congenial way of thinking about it that we can believe. The statement of the poem compels belief. What I am trying to show is how Stevens's theory issues in poetry, and that chaos is ordered for Stevens not in his systematic thought, but in compelling statements in given poems. It is statements of the order of "The Curtains in the House of the Metaphysician" of which one should think when Stevens speaks of believing in a fiction.

Ego and Reality

The characteristic movement of Stevens's thought as it is engaged in poetry may be described by two points of reference, the first taken from "Notes toward a Supreme Fiction," the second from "The Man with the Blue Guitar":

From this the poem springs: that we live in a place
That is not our own and, much more, not ourselves
And hard it is in spite of blazoned days.
    (*CP*, p. 383)

I am a native in this world
And think in it as a native thinks.
    (*CP*, p. 180)

Between these two points Stevens's thought flows as a current
between a negative and a positive pole. It is the gap between
them that the poem must bridge and that, in fact, creates the
need for the poem. In Stevens's theory it is the idea that after
the last negation an instinct for affirmation remains, that impels the movement from the first point to the second (see
"The Well Dressed Man with a Beard," *CP*, p. 247, and
"Esthetique du Mal," VIII, *CP*, pp. 319–20). The movement begins with the ego's sense of disconnection from the
absolute fact of reality that is felt as alien to the ego's concerns. As the ego approaches absolute fact it tends to reconcile that fact with its own needs through the imagination,
which thus establishes a vital connection between the ego and
reality. The absence of the imagination, or absolute fact,
must itself be imagined (*CP*, p. 503), and in the process the
fact is brought into meaningful relation with the ego. What
seemed inert, insubstantial, and irrelevant will then seem
vivid, substantial, and filled with interest. One will be as a
native who draws strength from his environment, rather than
an alien who is oppressed by it.

   This vivid sense of reality is produced by the imagination
and captured in some metaphor or description. At this phase
Stevens's poetry tends to be in praise and amplification of the
reality so imagined. But as the ego's idea of reality imposes it-

self in our apprehension of reality, it becomes a "violent order," a cliché that distorts reality and is a falsification of it. We then escape solipsism through a desire to return to absolute fact, to forsake our ideas about the thing for the thing itself, which at this point seems like "A new knowledge of reality" (*CP*, p. 534).

> . . . so poisonous
>
> Are the ravishments of truth, so fatal to
> The truth itself, the first idea becomes
> The hermit in a poet's metaphors,
>
> Who comes and goes and comes and goes all day.
>   (*CP*, p. 381)

Thus, an imbalance in favor of the imagination is restored by a return to reality, and the see-saw career of our idea of reality starts all over again.

At the heart of this interchange between the ego and reality is the effect of the imagination in bringing the two into vital relation. I suspect that this is not merely a point of theory for Stevens but rather an intensely real experience upon which the theory was constructed. Faced with the depressing prospect of a reality that seems dull, plain, and irrelevant to the needs of the ego, the poet comes to feel that the world in which he lives is thin and insubstantial, so remote from his concerns that feeling he is part of it "is an exertion that declines" (*OP*, p. 96). When, through the imagination, the ego manages to reconcile reality with its own needs, the formerly insipid landscape is infused with the ego's emotion and reality, since it now seems intensely relevant to the ego, suddenly seems more real.

It was everything being more real, himself
At the center of reality, seeing it.
It was everything bulging and blazing and big in itself.
    (*CP*, p. 205)

Stevens expressed this experience several times in more theoretical terms, as the manner in which the exercise of the
imagination gives us the sense of a vivid and substantial reality beyond the mind:

If we say that the space [reality] is blank space, nowhere, without
color, and that the objects, though solid, have no shadows and,
though static, exert a mournful power, and, without elaborating
this complete poverty, if suddenly we hear a different and familiar
description of the place:

This City now doth, like a garment, wear
The beauty of the morning, silent bare,
Ships, towers, domes, theatres, and temples lie
Open unto the fields, and to the sky;
All bright and glittering in the smokeless air;

if we have this experience, we know how poets help people to live
their lives.
    (*NA*, p. 31)

Again, in a passage on the function of poetry, abstracted by
Stevens from H. D. Lewis's article, "On Poetic Truth":[7]

Its function . . . is precisely this contact with reality as it impinges
on us from the outside, the sense that we can touch and feel a solid
reality which does not wholly dissolve itself into the conceptions of
our own minds . . . a quickening of our awareness of the irrevoca-
bility by which a thing is what it is, has such [particular] power, and
it is, I believe, the very soul of art.
    (*OP*, pp. 236–37)

The Function of the Imagination

The imagination for Stevens is not a way of creating, but of knowing. The imagination creates nothing, in the sense that it presents us with nothing that is not already in the world to be perceived. He in one place defines it as "the sum of our faculties," and characterizes it by its "acute intelligence" (*NA*, p. 61). He goes on to compare the imagination with light. "Like light," he says, "it adds nothing, except itself." The imagination, in other words, brings out meaning, enables us to see more. It does not create but perceives acutely, and the object of its perception is reality. What it perceives in reality is the credible. The credible, of course, is that which can be believed, and may be distinguished from absolute fact. The credible must be based on absolute fact, but is perceived by the imagination and may be beyond the range of normal sensibility (*NA*, p. 60). The nature of poetic truth is not that it is true in the sense that absolute fact is true, but that it says something about reality we can believe—which, of course, is not to say it is untrue. It moves us from a state in which we cannot believe something about reality to one in which we can believe something about reality, and consequently puts us, to use Stevens's phrase, in "an agreement with reality" (*NA*, p. 54).

Stevens writes that "the poet must get rid of the hieratic in everything that concerns him and must move constantly in the direction of the credible" (*NA*, p. 58). When a poet gives to us something about reality that we can believe which before had been incredible, he adds, again in Stevens's phrase, to "our vital experience of life" (*NA*, p. 65). The poem expresses that vital experience precisely because, as I have pointed out, in it the ego has reconciled reality with its needs so that reality is infused with the concerns of the ego. "A poem is a particular of life thought of for so long that one's thought has become an inseparable part of it or a particular of life so intensely felt that the feeling has entered into it" (*NA*, p. 65). The poet is able to add to our vital experience of life because of the heightened awareness of life that results from the intensity of his thought and feeling. In his essay "Three Academic Pieces," Stevens gives an example in another connection which is applicable here as illustration of the process of the imagination:

It is as if a man who lived indoors should go outdoors on a day of sympathetic weather. His realization of the weather would exceed that of a man who lives outdoors. It might, in fact, be intense enough to convert the real world about him into an imagined world. In short, a sense of reality keen enough to be in excess of the normal sense of reality creates a reality of its own. (*NA*, p. 79)

The poet, then gives us a credible sense of reality which brings us into vital relation with it.

Since the poet's vision is an intensified one, his description of reality in the poem is correspondingly heightened. It is "A little different from reality:/The difference that we make in what we see" (*CP*, p. 344). Here there is a pertinent analogy with Wordsworth, for whom the interaction of Nature and the imagination produced a new experience of reality resident in the poem. Stevens's idea is developed in "Description Without Place":

Description is revelation. It is not
The thing described, nor false facsimile.

It is an artificial thing that exists,
In its own seeming, plainly visible,

Yet not too closely the double of our lives,
Intenser than any actual life could be.
    (*CP*, p. 344)

Description is revelation in that it is an imaginative perception of the thing described: it is neither the thing itself, nor a
pretended reproduction of the thing. It is a new thing, not reality but a real artifice, so to speak, with its own reality that
makes actual reality seem more intense than it ordinarily is.
"The poem is the cry of its occasion,/Part of the res itself and
not about it" (*CP*, p. 473). The poem is not about the thing
(the "res"), but is the articulation of one's experience of the
thing, an experience in which the articulation—the writing of
the poem—is itself an essential part. To this should be added
Stevens's statement in "The Noble Rider and the Sound of
Words": "A poet's words are of things that do not exist without the words" (*NA*, p. 32).

With this in mind, regard a poem like "The Death of a Soldier" (*CP*, p. 97). The poem discovers a persuasive way of regarding a random and meaningless death as important and
dignified. It perceives something in the soldier's death, not
something that was not there in the fact of death, but something not seen except when looked at in a particular way, the
particular way the poem looks at it. This is the good of rhetoric, to provide the perception that comes through saying
things in particular ways.

The Function of Rhetoric

The sense of reality is given in poetry through what Stevens
calls "resemblance," or the similarities between things. The
imagination creates resemblance in poetry through metaphor (*NA*, p. 72). Poetry, through resemblance, makes vivid

the similarities between things and in so doing "enhances the sense of reality, heightens it, intensifies it" (*NA*, p. 77). Therefore, "The proliferation of resemblances extends an object" (*NA*, p. 78). This is one theoretical source for Stevens's preoccupation, in poetic practice, with variations rather than progressive form, for it follows that saying a thing in another way is not merely repetition but also an extension of the original statement. In his essay "Two or Three Ideas," Stevens translates the first line of Baudelaire's "La Vie Anterieure," "J'ai longtemps habité sous de vastes portiques," in three different ways:

A long time I lived beneath tremendous porches.
   (*OP*, p. 203)
I lived, for long, under huge porticoes.
   (*OP*, p. 203)
A long time I passed beneath an entrance roof.
   (*OP*, p. 213)

One of the points he is trying to make in doing so is that our sense of reality changes and that this change is reflected in terms of style by the way we say things about it. "The most provocative of all realities is that reality of which we never lose sight but never see solely as it is. The revelation of that particular reality or of that particular category of realities is like a series of paintings of some natural object affected, as the appearance of any natural object is affected, by the passage of time, and the changes that ensue, not least in the painter" (*OP*, p. 213–14).

For Stevens, poetry is a way of saying things in which the way of saying yields the meaning and in which the way of saying is more important than, but indistinguishable from, the thing said. "The 'something said' is important, but it is important for the poem only in so far as the saying of that par-

ticular something in a special way is a revelation of reality"
(*OP*, p. 237).[8] It is not only written language but also its
sound that gives us, in poetry, a credible sense of reality:
"words, above everything else, are, in poetry, sounds" (*NA*,
p. 32). We seek in words a true expression of our thoughts
and feelings which "makes us search the sound of them, for a
finality, a perfection, an unalterable vibration, which it is
only within the power of the acutest poet to give them" (*NA*,
p. 32). This kind of truth is that of true rhetoric: the appro-
priateness of a particular way of putting things is what persuades us of the truth of that way of putting things. True rhetoric, which is the poet's obligation, "cannot be arrived at by
the reason alone," and is reached through what we usually
call taste, or sensibility; hence Stevens speaks of the morality
of the poet as "the morality of the right sensation" (*NA*, p.
58). When the right sound is discovered, it gives pleasure:
when Stevens speaks of listening to the sound of words, he
speaks of "loving them and feeling them" (*NA*, p. 32). The
pleasure given by the right sound, apart from this sensuous-
ness of language, is that of the gratification that occurs when
the imagination, through language, brings one into a favorable adjustment to reality. "The pleasure that the poet has
there is a pleasure of agreement with the radiant and produc-
tive world in which he lives. It is an agreement that Mallarmé
found in the sound of *Le vierge, le vivace et le bel aujourd
'hui*" (*NA*, p. 57). Thus Stevens can regard language as a
god, a savior, in face of a bitter reality: "Natives of poverty,
children of malheur,/The gaiety of language is our seigneur"
(*CP*, p. 322). For Stevens, "There is a sense in sounds beyond their meaning" (*CP*, p. 352), and that sense of sound
beyond meaning is an essential of language as it is used in poetry.

Obscurity

Stevens does not hesitate to reduce or obscure the discursive meaning of the language he employs in order to get at that sense in sounds. That is why he writes, "The poem must resist the intelligence/Almost successfully" (*CP*, p. 350).[9] Again, he writes: "A poem need not have a meaning and like most things in nature often does not have" (*OP*, p. 177). This line of thought probably came to Stevens from the French Symbolist tradition, in which there is a conscious division between the creative and communicative functions of language,[10] and in which, therefore, the creative value of words depends on their suggestiveness rather than on their strict meaning, so that obscurity and lack of specificity become virtues. "[Poems] have imaginative or emotional meanings, not rational meanings. . . . They may communicate nothing at all to people who are open only to rational meanings. In short, things that have their origin in the imagination or in the emotions very often take on a form that is ambiguous or uncertain."[11] This would account for some of Stevens's obscurity as intentional, as I think is the case in the insistently cryptic "Thirteen Ways of Looking at a Blackbird." Certainly it could account for his freedom in coinage and, further, in his employment of nonsense. "I have never been able to see why what is called Anglo-Saxon should have the right to higgle and haggle all over the page, contesting the right of other words. If a poem seems to require a hierophantic phrase, the phrase should pass" (*OP*, p. 205). Usually Stevens's nonsense, while it has no rational meaning of its own, does create a meaning in its context which it communicates, as in "An Ordinary Evening in New Haven," XXIX, where the sound of the phrase, "the micmac" (also "intrigues" or "maneuvers" in French) "of mocking birds," in description of the lemons, helps to distinguish the character of "the land of the lemon trees" from that of the cloddish "land of the elm trees" (*CP*, p. 486). Frequently, however, Stevens's obscurity is not due merely to the use of language for effects that exclude rational meaning. Despite Stevens's calculated use of obscurity, his poetry has been from the beginning largely one of thought and statement. "Sunday Morning" is a meditative poem and in it, and in such poems as "The Comedian as the Letter C" and "Le Monocle de Mon Oncle," the initial and perhaps chief problem of explication lies in penetrating the rhetoric to determine the thought it contains. In the volumes following *Harmonium* the poetry, especially in the long poems, is increasingly discursive. It is evident both from his poetic practice and from his prose that Stevens came to hold the poetry of thought as an ideal:

Theoretically, the poetry of thought should be the supreme poetry. . . . A poem in which the poet has chosen for his subject a philosophic theme should result in the poem of poems. That the wing of poetry should also be the rushing wing of meaning seems to be an extreme aesthetic good; and so in time and perhaps, in other politics, it may come to be. It is very easy to imagine a poetry of ideas in which the particulars of reality would be shadows among the poem's disclosures. (*OP*, p. 187)

In fact, there is a sometimes unresolved division between the discursive and imaginative functions of language that exists throughout Stevens's poetry. "Thirteen Ways of Looking at a Blackbird" represents only one extreme of this division, at which it appears to be assumed that the communication of specific discursive meaning is incompatible with the esthetic effects of language. It is perhaps a sense of strain between the discursive and imaginative functions of language that moti-vates R. P. Blackmur's comment in his essay, "On Herbert Read and Wallace Stevens": "Does it not seem that he has always been trying to put down tremendous statements; to put down those statements heard in dreams? His esthetic, so to speak, was unaware of those statements, and was in fact rather against making statements, and so got in the way." [12] It is exactly this strain that makes itself felt when the referents of Stevens's language become uncertain, when his syntax fails, and his verse becomes unintelligible. Stevens uses obscurity in order to be suggestive, but he also uses it when the context requires that he be explicit. The blue and the white pigeons of "Le Monocle de Mon Oncle" are intelligible as contrasting states of mind and, though their meaning is indefinite, they suggest certain things about that contrast. But the "Blue buds or pitchy blooms" of "The Man with the Blue Guitar," XIII (*CP*, p. 172) seem to be specific kinds of intrusion into the blue of the imagination—a specific meaning for the phrase is implied, but is not communicated. The "three-four cornered fragrances/From five-six cornered leaves" of "An Ordinary Evening in New Haven," VIII (*CP*, p. 470), is in the same way puzzling rather than suggestive. On a larger scale, explication of section VI of the first part of "Notes toward a Supreme Fiction" (*CP*, p. 385) is problematic: a specific idea is indicated in the section but the statement fails to communicate it because the referent of the language is unspecified. One must guess at what is "not to be realized," what "must be visible or invisible." Sometimes uncertainty of meaning in Stevens's poems is caused by private reference, as in "The Man with the Blue Guitar," XV (*CP*, p. 173), which Stevens has glossed as referring to a popular song (*LWS*, p. 783). License for such private reference, however, comes out of his emphasis on the imaginative or creative aspect of language. If Stevens uses the phrase "dew-dapper clapper-traps" (*CP*, p. 182) to describe the lids of smoke-stacks (*MD*, p. 183), it is because he likes the way it sounds regardless of its obscurity. Unintelligibility in Stevens's poetry occurs characteristically when the communication of specific discursive content is frustrated by the use of those effects of language beyond meaning which Stevens conceives to be most essentially poetic.

Genre

As a poetry of thought and statement, that of Stevens has been compared with English neoclassical poetry. Stevens's poetry is not didactic, however, in the sense of arguing or discursively demonstrating its doctrine. In "The Man with the Blue Guitar" there is no consecutive argument and, though there is a kind of finale, no conclusion; and this is largely true of the long poems in the following volumes. These are poems that consist of nonsequential reflections on a central theme, in which the point of the poem is in the sum of the discrete reflections, in which conclusions are unimportant, in which, in fact, since if there is no progressive argument, there can be no logical conclusion. If they may be said to have a structure, it is fundamentally the structure of the poet's mind as it is realized in the act of improvisation. Hence on one hand the loose, limitless variations-on-a-theme form, as in "The Man with the Blue Guitar" or "An Ordinary Evening in New Haven," and on the other, the symmetrical but arbitrary forms, as in "Notes toward a Supreme Fiction," which serve as a frame within which to improvise. There is, for example, no formal reason why the three sections from *Opus Posthumous* (p. 72) called "Stanzas for 'The Man with the Blue Guitar,' " or even the poem, "Botanist on Alp (No. 2)" (*CP*, p. 135), could not be inserted in "The Man with the Blue Guitar" without harm to the whole.

Such poetry may be usefully distinguished from discursive or didactic poetry. In intent its end is not proof but conviction, or persuasion as in rhetoric except that it is as if Stevens were trying to persuade himself; its goal is not to demonstrate truth, but to effect resolution. It is aimed not at distinguishing the objective from the subjective, but at uniting the two (see "Extracts from Addresses to the Academy of Fine Ideas," VI). It does not attempt to assert fact, but rather seeks to adjust belief to fact, to bring about that "agreement with reality believed for a time to be true" (*NA*, p. 54) that Stevens conceives to be poetic truth. In other words its area of operation is not that of doctrine, but of psychology. That is why Stevens can write, "It is the belief and not the god that counts" (*OP*, p. 162), and again, "In the long run the truth does not matter" (*OP*, p. 180). For the dogmatist, for the philosopher, and for the didactic poet it is the truth that matters, and the adjustment to it is secondary. This is a poetry that adheres to a psychological mode of meditation whose end is resolution, as opposed to the discursive mode of the didactic whose end is demonstrated truth. It is therefore not surprising that Louis L. Martz finds that Stevens's poetry resembles formal Christian religious meditation.[13] But though he places Stevens in the meditative line of Donne, Herbert, and Hopkins, Stevens's resemblance to this line has nothing to do with form or tradition. On the contrary, the meditative character of Stevens's poetry is due to the untraditional ideological situation out of which he writes: he does not start with received truth that is to be justified as in, say, *Paradise Lost*, but from a position of no belief that constantly impels him to resolution in the repetitive search for the credible of which his poetry consists.

The Fiction

Stevens's clearest statement of the idea of a necessary fiction is in "Asides on the Oboe" (*CP*, p. 250):

The prologues are over. It is a question, now,
Of final belief. So, say that final belief
Must be in a fiction. It is time to choose.

However, in "Men Made out of Words" he writes that "Life consists/Of propositions about life" (*CP*, p. 355), then goes on to evoke the fear that our fictions, "the sexual myth,/The human revery or poem of death," are merely fictions, dreams, and that consequently, "defeats and dreams are one." And, in "The Pure Good of Theory" he declares:

Yet to speak of the whole world as metaphor
Is still to stick to the contents of the mind

And the desire to believe in a metaphor.
It is to stick to the nicer knowledge of
Belief, that what it believes in is not true.
    (*CP*, p. 332)

One must qualify the necessary fiction as a cardinal point in Stevens's thought with the idea that some such projection of the mind is not so much necessary as unavoidable. A major statement of this is in the Ozymandias fable of "Notes toward a Supreme Fiction": "A fictive covering/Weaves always glistening from the heart and mind" (*CP*, p. 396). Another is in "An Ordinary Evening in New Haven":

Inescapable romance, inescapable choice
Of dreams, disillusion as the last illusion,
Reality as a thing seen by the mind,

Not that which is but that which is apprehended,
A mirror, a lake of reflections in a room,
A glassy ocean lying at the door,

A great town hanging pendent in a shade,
An enormous nation happy in a style,
Everything as unreal as real can be.
    (*CP*, p. 468)

We never see merely what the eye takes in but compose as we see: "one looks at the sea/As one improvises, on the piano" (*CP*, p. 233). This, as stated in the poem "Variations on a Summer Day," accounts for such exercises in impressionism as "Sea Surface Full of Clouds." I do not wish to make Stevens consistent in a way in which he is not. With regard to the apprehension of reality, sometimes he says one thing and sometimes he says the opposite. In "An Ordinary Evening in New Haven," for example, he also writes,

We keep coming back and coming back
To the real: to the hotel instead of the hymns
That fall upon it out of the wind.
    (*CP*, p. 471)

But in sum it comes to this: we can apprehend the substance of reality through our metaphors of it, but only for a moment; even as we make contact with the real we turn it into the imaginary, which quickly degenerates into cliché (see "Notes toward a Supreme Fiction," first part, II and III, *CP*, pp. 381–82). Reality is the data of the ego, but that data is transformed by the ego in the version of reality captured by the poem or the fiction:

It is never the thing but the version of the thing:
The fragrance of the woman not her self,
Her self in her manner not the solid block.
    (*CP*, p. 332)

"To lose sensibility, to see what one sees," can be for Stevens a matter of spiritual destitution (*CP*, pp. 320-21). At the other extreme, to see one meaning only through a rigid system of thought is also spiritual poverty. The latter condition is personified in the figure of Konstantinov in "Esthetique du Mal." He is the "logical lunatic," "the lunatic of one idea/In a world of ideas," whose extreme of logic is illogical (*CP*, pp. 324-25). Fictions must be credible in the face of reality, and in fact the "pressure of reality" demands that we resist it with credible fictions (*NA*, pp. 22-23).

The fiction, so qualified, is a credible version of reality. It is neither reality itself nor a projection of the ego, but an abstract construction of the relation between the two in which the feelings of the ego are adjusted to the fact of reality. The fiction must be abstract because it must be selective in discovering those aspects of reality that meet the needs of the ego.[14] Thus a fiction is not belief in the ordinary sense but is a crystallized relation to reality that reveals reality as in some way gratifying to the ego—or, as the third subdivision title of "Notes toward a Supreme Fiction" tells us, it must give pleasure. Belief is a matter of "the more than rational distortion,/The fiction that results from feeling" (*CP*, p. 406).

We do not depend on poetry or a theory of belief to bring us into this relation with reality, for we are moved naturally into such experiences by fortuitous events in the world around us:

. . . when the sun comes rising, when the sea
Clears deeply, when the moon hangs on the wall

Of heaven-haven. These are not things transformed.
Yet we are shaken by them as if they were.
We reason about them with a later reason.
    (*CP*, pp. 398-99)

But "The casual is not/Enough" (*CP*, p. 397), so Stevens systematizes, through his theory, the specifications for this relation in order to be able to encourage it into existence. The success of this process is described with exactitude in "The Man with the Blue Guitar," XVIII (*CP*, p. 174), as it occurs "After long strumming on certain nights." A "dream"—a fiction which is not quite believable—when it becomes credible in face of reality, is no longer merely a fiction, a belief: "A dream no longer a dream, a thing/Of things as they are." As a belief it is not held as an intellectual construction, but has a reality like that of the wind whose sensory presence is its only meaning ("wind-gloss"). Thus, the end of belief comes down to a gratifying, sensuous experience of reality, an agreement with life rather than an idea about it, "the mere joie de vivre" (*LWS*, p. 793).[15] Sometimes in Stevens, belief is put as a vital instinct, a sense of reality we project onto absolute fact in the way that the vegetation of spring grows over reality's barren rock, as if in this respect we mimic the organic processes of nature because we are of its nature (see "Long and Sluggish Lines" and "The Rock," I and II). Belief, then, is a sense of reality in which, as in death in "Flyer's Fall" (*CP*, p. 336), "We believe without belief, beyond belief."

"The Center That He Sought Was a State of Mind"

In "An Ordinary Evening in New Haven," XXVIII, Stevens writes that, "If it should be true that reality exists/In the mind," then the theory of poetry—the theory of how to create reality in the mind—would be the life of poetry. One might even, he goes on, extemporize "Subtler, more urgent proof that the theory/Of poetry is the theory of life" (*CP*, pp. 485–86). Though we exist in reality we are bound by the mind, and thus it is not the nature of reality that matters so much as our sense of it, the sense of it that the imagination gives us. However, the favorable sense of reality that the imagination can produce, the "agreement with reality," is momentary:

For a moment final, in the way
The thinking of art seems final when

The thinking of god is smoky dew.
            (*CP*, p. 168)

These moments are for Stevens a radical experience [16] which, it would not be too much to say, all his theoretical poetry merely tries to recapture. In a world without other spiritual center, the occurrence of this experience provides a focus, or a "foyer," as it is put in "Local Objects" (*OP*, p. 111). It includes "The few things, the objects of insight, the integrations/Of feeling,"

That were the moments of the classic, the beautiful.
These were that serene he had always been approaching
As toward an absolute foyer beyond romance.
            (*OP*, p. 112)

The intellectual content of the experience is no further defined, either in this poem or elsewhere, because it has no definite intellectual content. The experience is fortuitous, since one does not know what objective content to seek: it is composed of "things that came of their own accord,/Because he desired without knowing quite what" (*OP*, p. 112).

This is the same problem of content for a native and contemporary ideal that Stevens raised in the early poem, "The American Sublime": "What wine does one drink?/What bread does one eat?" (*CP*, p. 131). The answer is that there is no sacrament because there is no deity, that the ideal has no definite content, and that the "ultimate good" is a certain subjective experience whose only reality is psychological. "The Final Soliloquy of the Interior Paramour" (*CP*, p. 524) describes the "ultimate good" as the world imaginatively perceived so that one loses consciousness of the self and becomes aware of an order which is in fact that of the imagination ("that which arranged the rendezvous"). The "miraculous" power of the imagination creates a condition that seems to be one of secular beatitude that occurs "Here, now." Finally the imagination is identified with God, without, however, asserting the reality of God. On the contrary, the reality of the experience is entirely psychological, since the power that caused it, the imagination, operates only "Within its vital boundary, in the mind." The "ultimate good" here, the spiritual focus, may be described in the words of the opening line of "Artificial Populations" (*OP*, p. 112): "The center that he sought was a state of mind,/Nothing more." This is not an experience that depends on an accession of knowledge, or on an intuition of some known principle, such as deity, assumed to exist beyond the mind. The poem rather describes a state of mind in which the world is experienced in a certain desirable way: "nothing has been changed except what is/Unreal, as if nothing had been changed at all" (*OP*, p. 117).

Stevens raised another question in "The American Sublime" when he asked with regard to the sublime: "But how does one feel?" (*CP*, p. 131). The question is pertinent since the ideal he pursues is a certain experience, and comes down to a way he sometimes feels. "The Final Soliloquy of the Interior Paramour" describes not a rational but an emotional experience: one has a sense of "a warmth,/A light, a power," and one "feels" an obscure order (*CP*, p. 524). The language here suggests that in this condition a sensuous experience of reality is paramount. So also in "As You Leave the Room" (*OP*, p. 116), the modification of the ego which is accompanied by an exaltation of mood, "an elevation," is the result of an intensely sensuous experience of reality in which the latter seems "something I could touch, touch every way."

The most thorough description of this central experience, which is in the first part of "Notes toward a Supreme Fiction" (*CP*, p. 386), begins by dispensing with that poem's abstract apparatus in favor of purely sensuous description: "It feels good as it is without the giant,/A thinker of the first idea." Perhaps, the poem continues, a true experience of reality depends not on such abstractions but on that sensuous relation with it during, for example, "a walk around a lake," when one becomes composed as the body tires and physical composure comes to be one with mental composure. At such times one is in an equilibrium, a state of "incalculable balances," that includes both the mind and one's surroundings. This is exactly that resolution through an "agreement with reality" that Stevens's poetry aims to create. It is a radical combination of mood and circumstance that is "Extreme, fortuitous, personal." It involves the beauty of random events in reality, which, in the words of "The Sense of the Sleight-of-hand Man" (*CP*, p. 222), "Occur as they occur": "Could you have said the bluejay suddenly/Would swoop to earth?" But above all it requires an intense sensuous awareness of reality that is beyond the range of systematic thought. Hence the conclusion of "The Sense of the Sleight-of-hand Man":

It may be that the ignorant man, alone,
Has any chance to mate his life with life
That is the sensual, pearly spouse.

At the same time one has a sense of lucidity, even of clairvoyance, because one grasps the "truth"; one perceives reality in its sensuous integrity, and is completely satisfied with it. Compared to this, the truth of intellectual abstraction seems hazy and remote. So we are told at the end of the description of the experience in "Notes toward a Supreme Fiction":

We more than awaken, sit on the edge of sleep,
As on an elevation, and behold
The academies like structures in a mist.

What is fundamental in these moments of relation is an acute awareness of existence itself, the palm, in "Of Mere Being," "Beyond the last thought," in which the golden bird sings and which is the end that we desire only for itself: it is this and "not the reason/That makes us happy or unhappy" (*OP*, pp. 117–18).[17] This is the sense of existence for which the ghosts yearn in "Large Red Man Reading":

They were those that would have wept to step barefoot into reality,
That would have wept and been happy, have shivered in the frost
And cried out to feel it again, have run fingers over leaves
And against the most coiled thorn, have seized on what was ugly
And laughed . . .
    (*CP*, pp. 423–24)

At the same time there occurs an agreement between the ego and reality in which the separation between the two disappears and they seem one harmonious entity: "The reader became the book," and "The quiet was part of the meaning, part of the mind" (*CP*, p. 358).[18] The reconciliation of the ego with reality produces a vivid and harmonious sense of existence.

Ultimately, one is brought to reality, and consequently brought to life, by one's feeling for reality; in such feeling lies the poem's power to revivify. The poet in "Large Red Man Reading" brings the ghosts to life because he "spoke the feeling for them, which was what they had lacked" (*CP*, p. 424). The possibility of such an experience of revivification, in which "being would be being himself again,/Being, becoming seeing and feeling and self" (*CP*, p. 255), is described in "Extracts from Addresses to the Academy of Fine Ideas," IV. Section V of that poem considers the possibility of an abstract idea that might make such experience generally available, but VI rejects systematic thought, and the poem finally places faith in imaginative expressions based on feeling, "The heart's residuum," for a positive relation with reality despite its inherent evil.

Since this experience of ideal relation with reality is by nature fugitive, there can be no formulation of it that one can repeat to summon it up; nothing avails but improvisation. And when improvisation fails, when the ego cannot bridge the gap between it and a too alien reality, there is an antithetical experience, a negative counterpart of the ideal one. It occurs when the relation to reality becomes too great a burden, so that "being part is an exertion that declines" (*OP*, p. 96). When this happens, the ego may attain composure by withdrawing from reality into itself, just as it may in opposite circumstances attain composure through heightened experience of reality. Thus in "Solitaire under the Oaks" (*OP*, p. 111), one escapes from reality to "pure principles" and is, consequently, "completely released." The point of the experience described in the poem is release, and though it is achieved through contemplation of principle, the principle is unimportant so long as it is instrumental in bringing about this release. What is desired is a state of mind, a psychological equilibrium without any particular intellectual content, in which one is relieved of the pressures of reality. Whereas the positive counterpart moved toward greater experience of reality, this state of mind seems to move toward exclusion of any experience of it: one exists in an "oblivion," thinking "without consciousness" about arbitrary principle, so that "Neither the cards nor the trees nor the air/Persist as facts." Instead of a heightened sense of existence, one finds here precisely its opposite: it is

As if none of us had ever been here before
And are not now: in this shallow spectacle,
This invisible activity, this sense.
    (*OP*, p. 113)

It is true, of course, that these are all late poems, and may represent a composed withdrawal from life in preparation for death, but one finds among the same group far more poems about the opposite experience, such as "The Final Soliloquy of the Interior Paramour" and "As You Leave the Room" (*OP*, p. 116), the latter of which seems quite plainly a poem whose occasion is the end of life. This negative experience is epitomized in "An Ordinary Evening in New Haven," XX (*CP*, p. 480):

. . . the pure sphere escapes the impure

Because the thinker himself escapes. And yet
To have evaded clouds and men leave him
A naked being with a naked will
And everything to make. He may evade
Even his own will and in his nakedness
Inhabit the hypnosis of that sphere.

The thinker may escape the real world ("the impure") for a consciousness pure of reality. But the evasion of any idea of reality creates the need for another to take its place ("everything to make"), unless the thinker manages to exclude all content from his consciousness (which may therefore be described as "his nakedness") and remains in a hypnotic state that, perhaps, resembles the extinction of consciousness in mystic nirvana or, perhaps, merely the point of inanition in revery. But one cannot sustain this state of mind any more than one can sustain its counterpart. There is a "will," a given in human nature that amounts to a necessity, in himself and others, that he must evade in order to enter this state and that he cannot evade for long, that drives the thinker's consciousness back into contact with reality once more. So the succeeding section (XXI) begins:

But he may not. He may not evade his will,
Nor the wills of other men; and he cannot evade
The will of necessity, the will of wills.

When either of these fugitive experiences is consummated, then, one moves toward its opposite. Here, undoubtedly, is a source of the characteristic polar fluctuation of Stevens's thought in its repetitive approach to and withdrawal from reality.

The Importance of Stevens's Art

One of the sayings in the group of comments called the "Adagia" runs as follows: "Life is an affair of people not of places. But for me life is an affair of places and that is the trouble" (*OP*, p. 158). The remark is apposite to Stevens's poetry. He did not write poetry that had to do with people in social relation. There is little in his poetry of narrative, little that is personal, little that is occasional, nothing that is dramatic. In an age before, as he put it, Marx ruined nature, he might have been a nature poet of the magnitude of Wordsworth. He wrote about his response to place, to objects, to landscape, and he wrote about ideas, and his ideas come down to the importance of an intense responsiveness not to personality, nor indeed to ideas, but to sensuous, physical reality. The essential self is, for him, the body,

The old animal,

The senses and feeling, the very sound
And sight . . .
     (*CP*, pp. 46–47)

In Stevens's vision, that which is beyond the self is a fluid, constantly changing present in which nothing endures and nothing has any end beyond itself:

It is a theatre floating through the clouds,
Itself a cloud, although of misted rock
And mountains running like water, wave on wave,

Through waves of light. It is of cloud transformed
To cloud transformed again, idly, the way
A season changes color to no end,

Except the lavishing of itself in change.
     (*CP*, p. 416)

In such a reality the effort of the intellect to discover absolute value seems absurd, and reality itself seems to lose its substance and solidity. Stevens appealed to the senses to give him, through poetry, a feeling of the substantiality of that reality beyond the mind as something pleasurably vivid, fresh, and various rather than same, insipid, and without value.

We do not have to be told of the significance of art. "It is art," said Henry James, "which makes life, makes interest, makes importance . . . and I know of no substitute whatever for the force and beauty of its process." (*NA*, p. 169)

1967

IV. Arguments

The New Tradition

Obviously there's no progress in art. Progress toward what? The avant-garde is a convenient propaganda device but when it wins the war everything is avant-garde which leaves us just about where we were before. The only thing that's sure is that we move, and as we move we leave things behind—the way we felt yesterday, the way we talked about it. Form is your footsteps in the sand when you look back. Art consists of the forms we leave behind in our effort to keep up with ourselves, define ourselves, create ourselves as we move along, like Malone dying or Genet in prison. Traditions, also, are after the fact. Traditions are inventions—a decision accumulates about which part of the museum is most useful to us in the ongoing present. Now and then a reorganization seems in order. We suddenly discover a kinship with Donne or Greek Antiquity. Pieces are moved up from the basement and dusted off, there's a major turnover in the catalogue, we "discover" Japanese art. It's hard to believe the novel has a future because, like certain people, it has the wrong kind of past. What we think of as the novel has lost its credibility—it no longer tells what we feel to be the truth as we try to keep track of ourselves. There's no point pushing ahead with fiction, we might as well write autobiography and documentary, or social criticism and other how-to books. But suppose fiction is something other than what we tend to think it is? I would like to propose the invention of a new tradition for fiction.

You can't manufacture a tradition with a whole body of work, its successes, its examples, its interconnections, its ways of thinking and proceeding. By definition it must already be there awaiting only one final element—that we say it exists. We have already had some work that talks about a new line of fiction as if it exists. Such people as Robert Scholes, Ihab Hassan, Hugh Kenner, and Alain Robbe-Grillet have already digested some of this material for us, and an important new book by Sharon Spencer talks about a very large group of modern novelists, many of them unfamiliar in this country, as if they had the coherence of a school. *Space, Time and Structure in the Modern Novel* (New York University Press, 1971) begins with a quote from Anaïs Nin's *The Novel of the Future*: "It is a curious anomaly that we listen to jazz, we look at modern paintings, we live in modern houses of modern design, we travel in jet planes, yet we continue to read novels written in a tempo and style which is not of our time and not related to any of these influences." There is no shortage of a renewed fiction, as Spencer's book amply demonstrates, and many of its examples have already gained a wide audience. The phenomenon of which Nin speaks is no longer a "curious anomaly"—it is simply a function of the economics of the publishing industry and a lagging criticism. Given the situation, the initial virtue of the Spencer book is its choice of subject. It responds to necessity. Fiction is one of the ways we have of creating ourselves and the lives we lead. We speak of a new fictive tradition as if it exists because we need to.

The first thing that must be said about the new tradition of the novel is that it's not modern. The modern is now a period—both an era and an end of something. It implies 1939, the New York World's Fair, the Trylon and Perisphere. The modern behaved as if a new age were due tomorrow, and as if it were it, the final goal of progress. Here in tomorrowland we have a more tragic sense of things. We know there's no such thing as progress, that a new age may be a worse one, and that since the future brings no redemption, we better look to the present. In consequence the new tradition makes itself felt as a presence rather than a development. Instead of a linear sequence of historical influences it seems a network of interconnections revealed to our particular point of view. Like Eliot's view of tradition, it would resemble a reservoir rather than a highway project, a reservoir that is ahistorical, international and multilingual. Our curriculum would probably start with *Don Quijote* in which we would note the split between the pragmatic and the fantastic, the empirical and the imaginative, the objective and the subjective, between meaning and feeling, finally, represented by Sancho and the Don. We would then use this split to illustrate the old novel's inception in a schizophrenia of the word and we would show how the realism descending from Sancho required an initial depoeticization. From here we would move to Rabelais as an example of how such dissociations in fiction can be avoided through the unity of a style that treats creation in both its senses as "all the same river." From Rabelais we might go almost anywhere—to encyclopedic multiplicity unified by wordplay in *Finnegans Wake*, or to Sterne via a joke borrowed from Rabelais in *Tristram Shandy*. In the case of *Tristram Shandy* we would point out how the new tradition coexisted with the old tradition from the beginning, not as the exception that proves the rule but as an alternative rule. We would then proceed to articulate the new tradition through groups of similar novels without regard to period or nationality. We would talk about the qualities common to each of these types of new fiction, qualities that in many cases they would share with other types within the tradition as a whole.

The Spencer book deals with one such type, in fact it creates the type—that is, the books were there (Butor, Cortázar, Nabokov, Nin, Musil, Robbe-Grillet, Gertrude Stein, Gide, many others) but the type wasn't before Spencer got hold of them. The "architectonic novel," as she calls it, is characterized by the spatialization of its form. The spatialization of form serves as an alternative to the old novel's sequential organization in plot and narrative. Through such techniques as juxtaposition and manipulation of the print on the space of the page, the novelist can create a structure which communicates by means of pattern rather than sequence in a manner approaching that of the plastic arts. This kind of writing— one immediately thinks of the prose of John Cage and Raymond Federman's *Double or Nothing*—can be taken in with something like the simultaneous apprehension of someone looking at a box in a comic strip. One model for a work of fiction is the jigsaw puzzle. The picture is filled out but there is no sense of development involved. When you feel that things are happening to you without logic or sequence this is a good model to use—situations come about through a cloudburst of fragmented events that fall as they fall and finally can be seen to have assumed some kind of pattern. The sequential organizations of the old novel are coming to seem like an extravagant, if comforting, artifice—things don't appear to happen according to Aristotle any more.

A novel is both a concrete structure and an imaginative structure—pages, print, binding containing a record of the movements of a mind. The form is technological, the content is imaginative. The old novel tends to deny its technological reality, but, as Spencer points out with reference to Hugh Kenner, the book is "a spatial phenomenon by its very essence." A canvas is flat: a painter may wish to affirm its flatness or deny it through perspective. A writer may wish to convey an illusion, an imitation of reality, or he may wish to create a concrete structure among the other concrete structures of the world, although one which, like a piece of music, may alter our perceptions of the rest. The novel as illusion is no longer credible, so why bother (Spencer might disagree). But if we treat the novel as a concrete technological structure there is no reason why we can't go ahead in that direction and try to improve the technological structure to suit the purposes of our imaginations. There is the example of the Frenchman Marc Saporta who has published a novel in a box so that its pages may be shuffled to read in various orders determined by chance. One can envision novels printed on scrolls, on globes, on moebius strips (see John Barth's *Lost in the Funhouse*), on billboards—or not printed at all but produced on electronic or video tape, or acted out on a stage. Beyond the frame is certainly one possible direction to go, though, as in the history of painting from cubism's "painting out" to the total displacement of the work of art into reality in the "happening," there is some indefinable line beyond which the art you are working in becomes some other art, or no art at all. Fine. Who's to say that painters can't put on plays, and if novelists want to try a little skywriting, that could be fun too. The other direction lies in acknowledgement of the nature of the medium, as in the history of American painting from

Gorky to Pop Art in painting "flat," which may permit as much exploitation of the genre without the danger of departure from it. A. R. Ammons wrote his poem *Tape for the Turn of the Year* on a roll of adding machine tape but, while retaining the resultant verse form, cut up the tape and published it in the pages of a book. The consequence is an interesting tension between the vertical thrust of the tape and the consecutive pull of the pages. The book contains the tape form and accommodates it to its own. To complain that the novel can't escape from its binding, as one critic does, is like complaining that the mind can't escape from its skull.

We badly need a new way of thinking about novels that acknowledges their technological reality. We have to learn how to look at fiction as lines of print on a page and we have to ask whether it is always the best arrangement to have a solid block of print from one margin to the other running down the page from top to bottom, except for an occasional paragraph indentation. We have to learn to think about a novel as a concrete structure rather than as an allegory, existing in the realm of experience rather than in the realm of discursive meaning, and available to multiple interpretation or none, depending on how you feel about it—like the way that girl pressed against you in the subway. Novels are experiences to respond to, not problems to figure out, and it would be interesting if criticism could begin to expand its stock of responses to the experience of fiction.

I presume that the movement of fiction should always be in the direction of what we sense as real. Its forms are expendable. The novelist accommodates to the ongoing flow of experience, smashing anything that impedes his sense of it, even if it happens to be the novel. Especially if it happens to be the novel. But it takes form to destroy form and a new form is highly noticeable. It's almost inevitable that a writer who is merely trying to get closer to his experience will at first be called self-conscious, formalistic, or literary. The kind of form employed by Laurence Sterne is, in this sense, still new to us. "Writing about writing," the critics like to sneer about this type of novel—too self-conscious. Nevertheless I'll bet that the multifaceted, antisequential, surrational *Tristram Shandy* is closer to the truth of your experience these days than is *Robinson Crusoe*. Sterne's calculated demolition of the conventions of "the" novel is a thrust into reality rather than a retreat into literature. Let's do away with make-believe, we aren't children. Why suspend disbelief—is Disneyland really necessary? It's as if we have to make believe before we can work up the confidence to believe, as if belief in good conscience were the privilege of primitives or maybe Europeans. Disney, like Coleridge, found an excuse to escape statistics, but Sterne knew we never needed an excuse.

One slogan that might be drawn from Sterne's anti-art technique is that, instead of reproducing the form of previous fiction, the form of the novel should seek to approximate the shape of our experience. In this respect and in many others, Diderot's ignored masterpiece, *Jacques the Fatalist*, which literally begins and ends with *Tristram Shandy*, is the direct descendant of Sterne. In its emphasis on the act of composition, among other things, Gide's *The Counterfeiters* has much in common with Sterne and Diderot on the one hand and Genet and Beckett on the other. And of course there is Viktor Shklovsky's great novel of the Russian Revolution, *A Sentimental Journey*, translated only last year, which is as deeply indebted to Sterne as is Diderot's *Jacques*. The Russian Formalist's book, in turn, has many similarities with *The Counterfeiters*, especially in its technique of "retardation," which comes to much the same thing as Gide's intentional destruction of continuity. Perhaps the fundamental assumption behind this line of fiction is that the act of composing a novel is basically not different from that of composing one's reality, which brings me back to a slogan I draw from Robbe-Grillet's criticism that the main didactic job of the contemporary novelist is to teach the reader how to invent his world. Writers like Genet, Beckett, and Nabokov, especially in *Pale Fire*, move away from the pretence of imitation and representation to pure and undisguised invention.

There have to be many ways for fiction to deal with the multiplicity of experience, and still another live alternative to "the" novel might be grouped around the axis of Kleist, Kafka, and Borges. If Borges is like a Kafka without anguish, then another important but little known novelist who can be associated with this line, Raymond Roussel, is like Kafka without anything, a castle without a moat, without walls, without buildings—an absence. *The Castle* can be read as an allegory of everything; Roussel's *Impression of Africa* reads like an allegory of nothing, gratuitous inventions, puzzles solved by further puzzles, insignificance explained by what turns out to be even less significant until, as with Kafka, one is driven out of the depths back to the cryptic surface of experience that exists despite interpretation and beyond interpretation. The connection with the French "new novel" is clear, especially with Sarraute and Robbe-Grillet–Butor having moved off into the architectonic mode. With a twist of the surreal in the direction of the fantastic you arrive at Donald Barthelme, and with another twist in the direction of the psychological you come to John Hawkes. Somewhere in this area you also find Leonard Michaels, Ishmael Reed, and, lately Jonathan Baumbach, as well as Kenneth Patchen, whose *Journal of Albion Moonlight* is another excellent book elbowed out of the way by "the" novel. Here also, and especially in connection with this line's recoil from the idea of profundity, you might run across Witold Gombrovicz, whose *Pornografia* reads like an eroticized Henry James, with all the latter's suppressed devils unchained and raging.

There are two important types of modern fiction that disappeared almost completely during the literary depression of the forties and fifties, although in this case we tend to bury them with critical lip service. "The revolution of the word," as they used to call the Paris experiments of Joyce, Stein, and the Surrealists, is probably still the crucial element in a renewed fiction, and the one least reckoned with by contemporary novelists. The reason it is crucial is that it deals with the nature of language itself, and any art, after all the other things it may be about, is fundamentally about its medium. Both the impossibly overloaded punning in *Finnegans Wake* and the impossibly opaque wordplay in Stein's *Tender Buttons* raise the question of whether it is really the pragmatic, discursive, rationally intelligible side of language that best puts us in touch with our experience of the world and of ourselves. All writers are in love with nonsense as the water in which everyone swims, and Rimbaud's desperate assertions as well as Mallarmé's desperate negations are the extreme strategies of lovers attempting union with our native element. John Ashbery wrote recently that there are two ways of going about things: one is to put everything in and the other is to leave everything out. Joyce tends to put everything in and Gertrude Stein tends to leave everything out, and they both arrive at enigma. The only way to confront an enigma is to leave behind what you know in the hope of discovering something that you don't—understanding requires a release from understanding.

The other important line that was almost completely submerged during the counter-revolution of the oldfangled is that descending from D. H. Lawrence through Henry Miller and Anais Nin. After Lawrence's first impact as a sexual iconoclast it came to be recognized that his real subject was the crisis of the modern psyche and I believe the same shift is due to come about with respect to Miller's reputation. These writers are primarily psychological novelists. I think of their books as wisdom books, more analagous to *Job* or *Ecclesiastes* than to what we ordinarily think of as fiction, and of course Lawrence consciously made use of the gospel form. People read such books to find out how they should live their lives, and they are often very popular with the young, who presumably need most to find out. Hesse and Brautigan, for example, are also more or less in this line. The books of Carlos Castaneda, which though not novels have the texture and style of fiction, quite specifically transmit the wisdom of Castaneda's teacher, the medicine man Don Juan. They remind me of Hassidic and Sufic teaching stories, but unfold with the advantage of the novel's sophisticated techniques for rendering experience. The recent popularity of the autobiographical form may be attributed partly to the need for such books—as well as to the general voracious and often misguided appetite for facts—though the quality of recent autobiography (as well as of the "documentary novel") seems to depend on what kind of novel it happens to be imitating. Nin's *Diaries*, on the other hand, seem to be a counterpart to and a completion of her novels, and may in fact be her best novel.

One could go on to speak of other alternatives—the revitalization of narrative in the exuberant inventions of writers like John Barth and Gabriel García Márquez, or the work of the mythmakers and fairytalers like William Gass and Robert Coover. Such types are approximate and arbitrary anyway, though one's need to define them from a particular point of view is not. I prefer instead to cut the pie another way, and make note of a new thing that has recently been spotted from my observation post in California, where I and my students in the M. F. A. program in writing at the university where I taught a while were suddenly struck by many similarities in the fiction we were writing, in the fiction that was being submitted in applications from all over the country, and in certain writers of growing reputation. This new thing is a style that we have come to call the Bossa Nova, an elaboration of the new tradition. Needless to say the Bossa Nova has no plot, no story, no character, no chronological sequence, no verisimilitude, no imitation, no allegory, no symbolism, no subject matter, no "meaning." It resists interpretation because it doesn't want to be interpreted, but is very easy to understand once you forget about analyzing it. The Bossa Nova is nonrepresentational—it represents itself. Its main qualities are abstraction, improvisation, and opacity. The degree of abstraction may be great, as in Donald Barthelme, a writer who is very bossanova, or it may be slight as in Douglas Woolf, whose fiction seems to hover a fraction of an inch above the level of common experience, just enough to show that no experience is ever common. Woolf, who is in other respects not very bossanova, is nevertheless different enough to have been shouldered aside by "the" novel—or is it just that we can't tolerate anything serious in fiction unless it's dull or comes from Europe. His *Wall to Wall* and especially *Fade Out*, which is a kind of geriatric *Huckleberry Finn*, should be enough to get him generally recognized as one of the best writers going.

The best contemporary example of improvisational style that I know is the fiction of Steve Katz, a leading Bossanovan, who writes like a seal with the ball continually about to fall off its nose. He is a surfer on the wave of chaos and the closest thing to Rabelais since Rabelais, but try to find a man on the street who has read *The Exagggerations of Peter Prince* or

Creamy and Delicious and you will probably be taking a long walk. As abstraction frees fiction from the representational and the need to imitate some version of reality other than its own, so improvisation liberates it from any a priori order and allows it to discover new sequences and interconnections in the flow of experience. In a situation where traditional patterns of order seem false or superfluous it may be better to open oneself as completely as possible to the immediacy of experience and allow, in William Carlos Williams' phrase, "nothing that is not green." One way of doing this is through collage, which in fact Williams uses extensively in *Paterson*, and which Paul Metcalf, a descendant of Melville, puts to similar use in a fascinating and forgotten novel published in 1965 called *Genoa*, and in *Patagoni*, published in 1971.

Rudolph Wurlitzer is a writer whose work gets very close to the quality that I have in mind when I speak of opacity. His novels have the interesting effect of passing through your mind in the way icecream passes over your tongue—you get the taste and that's it. The experience exists in and for itself. It is opaque the way that abstract painting is opaque in that it cannot be explained as representing some other kind of experience. You cannot look through it to reality—it is the reality in question and if you don't see it you don't see anything at all. This quality, which is perhaps most brilliantly managed in Eugene Wildman's work and in some of Barthelme's stories, is a good antidote for that way we have of fending off experience by explaining it. Opacity implies that we should direct our attention to the surface of a work, and such techniques as graphics and typographical variation, in calling the reader's attention to the technological reality of the book, are useful in keeping his or her mind on that surface instead of undermining it with profundities. The truth of the page is on top of it, not underneath or over at the library.

Admittedly the Bossa Nova is nothing but a hopeful fabrication. In fact the whole paradoxical idea of a "new tradition" for fiction is a mere product of the imagination. Still who knows but that one day you may look up to find that a writer as peculiar as Jerzy Kosinski has won the National Book Award, or that Richard Brautigan's far out fables have become best sellers, or even that such esoteric artists as Beckett and Agnon have been awarded the Nobel Prize, and you may begin to wonder if something is happening Mr. Jones.

1972

Castaneda: Upward and Juanward

Everything happens and everything that happens is part of the story and everything that everyone thinks about what happens is part of the story and *Journey to Ixtlan* is part of Carlos Castaneda's story about Don Juan's story and this is my story about Carlos Castaneda's story.

My story begins as I was finishing another story a few years ago, the very last sections of my new novel, *Out*. At that time I happened to read the first published excerpt from Castaneda's second book, *A Separate Reality*, and I was astonished to find a number of similarities in incident and idea between *Out* and Castaneda's story. The more so in that the things in *Out* most parallel to Castaneda's book came out of my dreams, on which I have come to draw heavily in my writing. How could such a thing have happened, I wondered, unless I were a sorcerer or Castaneda a novelist—alternatives I have good reason to think equally absurd, Joyce Carol Oates, though I have to admit that the possibility of Don Juan being a kind of new Ossian presented itself strongly at first.

The mystery only deepened when I read the whole of *A Separate Reality* and found still more similarities, as in fact I continue to find them in *Journey to Ixtlan*. Shortly after this I discovered from Anaïs Nin that Castaneda lived and taught in Los Angeles near which I live, and she offered to invite him to her house so we could meet. The fact that this happened through Nin is an important part of the story. It was Nin who helped Castaneda publish *The Teachings of Don Juan* when he was having publisher troubles. And it is Nin more than any other writer I can think of who has over the years insisted on the continuity of dream and reality, as does Don Juan, and whose theories about fiction as controlled dreaming provide such a precise counterpart of Don Juan's ideas about learning to control one's dreams. Isn't it interesting how in stories everything comes together but to continue.

One of the first things I talked about with Castaneda when we met was the novelistic quality of his books. I told him frankly that as a novelist the first thing that occurred to me when I noticed the similarities between our books was that he too must be writing a novel. Since Joyce Carol Oates's letter to the *New York Times Book Review* raising the same possibility, I understand this must be a natural speculation for novelists and perhaps for others.

Castaneda, when I first met him two years ago, was rather different from the way he is now, and the change in him reflects the course the books have taken. That evening he struck me as a kind of Candide parrying with a schizophrenic episode, and in fact a kind of cultural schizophrenia—parallel to what one might call the controlled pathology induced by Don Juan—has been the key to his books since the first one, with its experiential reportage in the body of the book, and its attempt at an abstract objective analysis added on at the end.

His rather sturdy, Indian-looking face (he comes from South America where many people, I suppose, have Indian blood) seemed split into halves and his eyes seemed to go off in different directions. He looked like someone who had been holding himself together under enormous strain. Compounding his Candide demeanor with the signs of a struggling psyche, it struck me as impossible that anthropological forgery could have been a matter of concern for him or even of attention. He was not surprised at the similarities between my novel and his reportage, not even at the fact that my main source for them was my dreams. He said that there was a common fund of such knowledge that could be tapped by different people in different ways and that one of the ways was through dreams. He seemed to have in mind something like a lost Jungian race heritage. He also told me on that occasion stories about Don Juan that I have since heard him tell again and that appear in *Journey to Ixtlan* in somewhat less intimate detail, and which have the cumulatively convincing smell of experience rather than imagination.

Finally I don't really believe Castaneda could write a sustained work of pure imagination. One of his great virtues as reporter-sorcerer's apprentice, equally apparent in his work and in his person, is his stubborn literal-mindedness, so useful as a foil in bringing out Don Juan and in giving us a careful account of what happens between them.

On the other hand, to return to our conversation, not to further mystify what is already mysterious, grounds for a few, though not most, of the similarities between our stories can be located in my own experience, in that I had been impressed with a Sioux medicine man I met in South Dakota while I was writing *Out* and had been reading about the beliefs and practices of the Plains Indians, which are in some ways like those of the Mexican Indians.

However, once having said this, I have to confess that being overly concerned with the factuality of Castaneda's account seems in itself literal-minded. Castaneda is a visionary and in what sense does one ask whether a vision is "true"? A vision is beyond the category of fact, other than the fact of its having happened at all. Like a story, it is neither true nor false, only persuasive or unreal, and I think there are few people who would argue that Castaneda's accounts of his experience are not persuasive, as persuasive in fact as the most accomplished novels. Our culture likes to think of everything as true or false—this is a way it has of fending off enormous realms of experience that make us feel uneasy, and rightly so. The unknown must be explained and explained until it is explained away and we don't have to be afraid any more. We have to understand everything. It never seems to occur to anybody that the unknown is not merely dangerous but is also a momentous source, that it is the fertile medium in which we live, but such is the hysterical strength of our commitment to statistics.

Part of the enormous impact of Castaneda's books is due to the fact that they come at a time when this commitment is beginning to crumble in many quarters, when the empirical tradition has come to appear obviously inadequate, and the fact that Don Juan's teachings have so many similarities with Zen, with *The Book of the Dead*, with witchlore, with Sufism, with various Eastern disciplines, with the Western mystical tradition, with Jungian speculations, and perhaps most interestingly with Wilhelm Reich and his followers, only indicates that Castaneda is part of an important subplot in the story of the culture, and in stories, as I said, everything comes together. A major peripeteia is about to come off: what seemed true begins to lose credibility, and the incredible looks more and more likely.

Part of this cultural turnabout is the discovery that all accounts of our experience, all versions of "reality," are of the nature of fiction. There's your story and my story, there's the journalist's story and the historian's story, there's the philosopher's story and the scientist's story about what happens in the atomic microcosm and the cosmic macrocosm (scientists have a corner on the stories of creation and genesis these days). The scientist's version can be used to affect reality, you say—but so does a newspaper story or a poem or a piece of music, and so, it seems, does the power of a sorcerer. "For a sorcerer," says Don Juan in *Ixtlan*, "reality, or the world we all know, is only a description."

This is the key statement in all of Don Juan's teachings, and is also crucial, I believe, for our particular cultural moment. The secret of the sorcerer's power, it follows, is to know that reality is imagined and, as if it were a work of art, to apply the full force of the imagination to it. The alternating descriptions of reality that Don Juan works with are possible only by working through, and on, the imagination. His ordinary view of the world is only a description, Don Juan tells Castaneda, "a description that had been pounded into me from the moment I was born." Don Juan's whole effort is to disrupt Castaneda's description of the world, to "interrupt the normal flow of interpretation" (what Don Juan calls "not doing"), to "stop the world."

Every serious artist will immediately appreciate what Don Juan is trying to teach his seemingly unimaginative pupil. All art deconditions us so that we may respond more fully to experience, "to the perceptual solicitations of a world outside the descriptions we have learned to call reality," as Castaneda puts it. Don Juan is trying to get Castaneda to accept "the basic premise of sorcery," which is "that our reality is merely one of many descriptions." The fact, as it emerges more clearly in this book than in the preceeding ones, that Don Juan uses fear, trickery, deceit, hypnotism, and, least important in *Ixtlan*, drugs to accomplish this is totally beside the point.

Don Juan is Prospero. The world of the sorcerer is a stage and in Castaneda's books Don Juan is the skillful stage manager. What he is trying to teach Castaneda is not the primacy of one description over another, but the possibility of different descriptions. He is teaching Castaneda the art of description. And in so doing he breaks down, for the alert reader, that false separation of art from life, of imagination from reality that in our culture tends to vitiate both. This lost connection, which is the essence of primitive cultures, is maintained in our empiricist civilization only in the arts, where it is allowed to survive as in a zoo—in the zoo of the arts—and in witchcraft, the mystical cults, the various incursions of Oriental disciplines.

Once philosophy was stories, religion was stories, wisdom books were stories, but now that fiction is held to be a form of lying, even by literary sophisticates, we are without persuasive wisdom, religion, or philosophy. Don Juan shows us that we live in fictions, and that we live best when we know how to master the art. Fiction is the master art, Tom Wolfe, and journalism is a minor branch thereof. The sorcerer, the artist, sees beyond any particular form fiction may take to the fictive power itself, and in the absence of powerful fictions in our lives, maybe it's time for all of us to become sorcerers.

Not that I mean to imply that there's no difference between a sorcerer and an artist. Of course there is. For a sorcerer his life is his art and there is no product of it but himself.

The next time I saw Castaneda, to return to our story, was many months later when he came to lecture at the university where I was teaching at the time, and I went to talk to him for a while afterward. I was strongly impressed by a change in his bearing. He was much more together, more animated and cheerful, stronger, and there was nothing of the Candide left in him. In answer to a question, he had spoken about his fellow sorcerer-apprentices as jovial, practical, down-to-earth men, and I remember thinking how appropriate the description was to Castaneda himself. To know Castaneda is to be persuaded of the validity of his books—he is much like the consequence of the discipline he describes.

On that occasion I tried to draw him out on the resemblances between what he was involved with and the processes of the imagination in art, but his conception of art seemed a rather crude one, amounting to something like an idea of decoration. But if Castaneda's works aren't novels they're still stories, Castaneda's story about Don Juan's story, and I keep thinking of them in connection with other stories that explore similar areas for our culture.

In *Journey to Ixtlan*, for example, Castaneda, wandering through the Mexican mountains amid a landscape animated by spirits and powers, reminds me exactly of the early Wordsworth wandering in the English hills that are alive with immanent spirit. Or how about another Hispanic sorcerer, Cervantes, Castaneda's Sancho Panza to Don Juan's Quixote. Except that in this version of the story all the power is on the Don's side, which leads us to the thought that maybe Quixote was right all along, that maybe the culture, not to mention the novel itself, has conceded too much to the pragmatic Sancho.

Here it is Sancho Castaneda who undergoes the conversion, who finally has to admit that the windmills are giants, and that he has to struggle with them. Here it turns out that the Don is sane after all and the rest of us are mad, or if not mad at least gross dullards. These are works of art, Ms.

Oates, to answer your question directly, but works of art don't have to be novels. They are works of art compared, say, with Tom Wolfe's account of Kesey in *The Electric Kool-Aid Acid Test*, not because one is factual and the other is not, but simply because Castaneda's books attain a high level of imaginative power and coherence, of precision in language, of inventive selection, and Wolfe's book does not, though it may be an exemplar of the new journalism.

Must we really wait on the testimony of anthropologists about the value of these books? If the anthropological establishment were to rise up and cry fraud—and since it hasn't by now one can be certain it's not going to—wouldn't that, in a way, be even more exciting in imaginative terms?

When Joyce writes about forging the conscience of his race, I think he means "forge" in all of its senses. Gide understood that all art is counterfeit, even realistic art; this being so, why are American artists so guilty about the imagination? We should not need an old wizard, O Humanities Departments, to remind us of its scope and power. What's happened to our faculties? Why do we have to keep on saying the giants are, of course, really windmills, when the only important thing about them, as far as we're concerned, is that they're really giants? For Don Juan truth and lies are both unreal—the only thing that's real is knowledge.

Knowledge but not understanding. Don Juan speaks of "the absurdity of trying to understand everything." "The world is a mystery," he tells Castaneda. "Don't tax yourself trying to figure it out." With knowledge one is able to create a plausible description of that mystery. For that you need what Don Juan calls "personal power." Power is a feeling, according to Don Juan, "something like being lucky." In fact, for Don Juan "the world is a feeling," so one might say that the power of a sorcerer is the power of the feeling he can invest in his description so it is felt as a persuasive account of the world. As Castaneda comes to accept Don Juan's description of the world: there are spirits in waterholes, he can turn into a crow, Mescalito lives. What I find extraordinary here is the idea of feeling as a way of acting on the world, just as the forces we know through the physical sciences act on it. Feeling is neglected not only as a response in our culture but as an efficacious force, a power, though of course we see it acting every day and it is the effective force in the imaginative arts, in the imagination itself. It is, for example, the power that George McGovern didn't have and the Kennedys did. Feeling is the secret of power and the body is its medium: "I could not put the discovered secret into words, or even into thoughts, but my body knew it." Don Juan tells Castaneda that what he learns from him he learns with his body: "every time you have seen me your body has learned certain things, even against your desire." It is as if what Don Juan is teaching him is the wisdom of the body, the forgotten wisdom of animals that we have put out of consciousness and must now reintegrate.

Since I read that first excerpt from *A Separate Reality* I felt I had something to talk about with Castaneda, and, as I say, in stories everything comes together. First we met, then he came to lecture at the school where I was teaching last year, and finally he came to teach at that school and we had another chance to talk. One day Castaneda was good enough to come to a class I was teaching to discuss one of his books. One thing that was apparent then was his great caution in making claims about his apprenticeship to Don Juan, or "the field work" as he calls it. He seemed to feel that the very nature of his situation as participant-observer called for great caution in his account of it. When I pointed out that his situation enabled him to do something of unique value, that is, to describe the discipline of a sorcerer from both anthropological and subjective points of view, to both experience it and write about it, he replied first of all that Don Juan could produce a perfectly rational account of sorcery if he wanted to, and second, that there might come a time when he himself, Castaneda, might no longer want to write about it.

He was stubbornly indifferent to any similarities between his experience with Don Juan and Zen or any other discipline—that wasn't his concern. He was insistent—as he is in *Ixtlan*—that drugs are not at all an essential part of the apprenticeship and he spoke of a fellow apprentice he knew who had taken peyote only once and yet was far ahead of him as a sorcerer.

At that time he had already seen Don Juan for the last time in his apprenticeship, which is where *Ixtlan* leaves off. He was a powerful presence and, also, or maybe because, he really had his feet on the ground. Nevertheless I still sensed a split, not in him this time but in his effort to bridge two opposing cultures.

There was a lot I still wanted to talk about with Castaneda, but while he taught at the university he became increasingly elusive. Part of it no doubt was that there was a kind of mob scene with the students, but I think what he was really doing was emulating Don Juan in "dropping one's personal history," as it is put in *Ixtlan*. This is another strategy of the sorcerer, to increase his power: "if you have no personal history," Don Juan says, "no explanations are needed; nobody is angry or disillusioned with your acts. And above all no one pins you down with their thoughts."

What this finally amounts to is living totally in the present, concentrating one's power totally on the present rather than wasting it on the past and future. Don Juan believes one should behave as if each act were one's last on earth. This is something that Castaneda, in *Ixtlan*, is reluctant to do: "happiness for me was to assume that there was an inherent continuity to my acts . . . my disagreement was not a banal one but stemmed from the conviction that the world and myself had a determinable continuity."

Nevertheless, that is perhaps the direction in which, as a sorcerer, he is heading. He became notoriously hard to locate. He would claim to be going one place and mysteriously end up in another. You would expect to meet him here and you would find him there. I once went to meet him for a lunch appointment and was told by his colleagues and several other people that they knew for a fact he was in Mexico—when one of them met him in the elevator an hour or so later, he thought he was having a hallucination. Another time it was reported to me that he had abruptly left a line of students outside his office and disappeared, exclaiming that he had to speak to me right away—I never heard from him. More recently there was even a rumor that he was dead.

The best way to meet him was by accident. And that, in fact, is how I met him last, in a coffee shop in Los Angeles (neither of us is teaching now) after a talk by—we are apparently approaching the end of the story—Anaïs Nin. However, there was no chance for conversation because it was not the place and because, as he said, looking me straight in the eye, "I'm in Mexico." Then in explanation: "I go back and forth very fast. Why don't you get in touch next time you're in Los Angeles," he added. "We should talk." So there's still another conversation I've been wanting to have with Castaneda, and this is it.

If the way of the sorcerer lies in the direction of utter detachment then I have a final question. Don Juan and Don Genaro at the end of *Ixtlan* are seen to be magnificent but terribly lonely and isolated men. They have dropped out of the human community and their only community is that of other sorcerers. This is Castaneda's most unillusioned book and the two master brujos are to this extent demystified. But even Prospero throws down his staff.

It occurs to me that there are two ways to go about things on the journey to transcendence—either bring the human baggage along or leave it behind. As in the mystic tradition Don Juan leaves it behind. He has power but he is empty. It seems to me that it would be preferable to bring it along, and that the more you can bring along the better. That's what makes the difference between a saint and a mere ascetic, I suppose. And I suppose the greatest saint would bring along not only all his own baggage but everyone else's as well, and by the passion of his involvement with the human community would become a prophet: Moses, Christ, Gandhi.

Don Juan goes the other way: personal power, personal composure, at the price of withdrawal from the community, an awesome isolation, a contained nostalgia. Given the community maybe it's the only way out, but I hope not. Is that one single sorcerer who won the struggle with his ally and so retained his humanity the only one able to maintain a continuity with those he has left so far behind? Is even he able to do it?

What do you think, Carlos?

1973

Reprinted with permission of the author and The Village Voice © *1973.*

Writing on Writing

I. Robert Creeley

At some point Kenneth Koch, I think, remarked on the problem of having your artistic career depend on people who have no idea what you're doing, an observation which immediately leads to the question of whether there is, today, a viable criticism by writers who presumably know what other writers are doing, and to the further question of whether there is a poetics plausible to poets and fiction writers. Anyone interested in these things should look at Robert Creeley's collection of essays, *Was That a Real Poem* (Bolinas: Four Seasons Foundation, 1979), which not only contains innumerable insights about writing, but maybe more important, demonstrates a style of commentary appropriate to contemporary art and implies an alternative to the terminologically occult, theoretical kind of commentary now popular in academic circles. What we get in Creeley is an insistence on the experience of composition in a style that is, therefore, scrupulously deformalized, provisional, and reluctant to come to conclusions except in "my own terms of experience," the experience of writer as writer which is his expertise. "What I deny, then, is any assumption that that order [of poetry] can be either acknowledged or gained by intellectual assertion, or will, or some like intention to shape language to a purpose which the literal act of writing does not itself discover."

The result, then, is an antisystematic form of commentary serving an area of discourse in which no predetermined procedure is desirable, that moves the way the mind moves, erratically, provisionally, the way Klee talks of taking the line for a walk, like a walk around the lake, as Wallace Stevens says somewhere, or by digression, as Sterne would put it. The texture of the essays—filled with phrases like, "A friend recently told me here of a book he'd been reading wherein . . ."; "Gary Snyder tells me that . . ."; "I think that where my own confusion lies . . ."—demonstrates thinking as the experience of persons rather than the prerogative of professionals. "The human event must be permitted to enter, again, the most significant of its own self-realizations." As an imprint of "the human event" ("the act of the mind" as Stevens put it), the writing is insistently unpolished or, at another level, the antidote to slick. " 'How can we tell the dancer from the dance,' " Creeley quotes Yeats and responds, "Who was it that wanted to," here coming out of the other side of Modernism, Flaubert's irony of indifference, Joyce like a god above his creation paring his fingernails, down to the New Criticism's quarantine of art from life, and especially from the artist's life.

Writing, here, is seen as agency, a *process* summoning up those unpremeditated events that occur in the field of composition, in which the writing itself, the intervention of "the measure," is one of the variables. "I have never explicitly known—before writing—what it was that I would say." "I want to give witness not to the thought of myself—that specious concept of identity—but, rather, to what I am as simple agency." The writer is a medium, in several senses, and his text is the ongoing notation of his agency—the medium catalyzes the message. Negative capability as opposed to the egotistical sublime, the megalomania of Pound's "ego-system," as Olson names it, that forces everything into a premeditated mould. The mind must remain open to the unknown, to what it does not yet understand, to the disorder of experience. A recent study proposes that artists have a higher tolerance for disorder than others because, Creeley suggests, "poets among others involved in comparable acts have an intuitive apprehension of a coherence which permits them a much greater admission of the real, the phenomenal world." Experience is larger than the intellect as it is usually conceived, and part of the poet's responsibility is that "the elemental nature of existence *not* be lost in the thought of it." Thinking is part of being but does not define it, and is one of the variables in the *act* of writing along with the presumed subject, considerations of energy, chance, form, and so on, an act as complex as the experience it addresses because it is part of the experience it addresses. And conversely, part of the poem is the experience of writing it, in the sense that a Pollock painting is a record of its own composition. One of the striking things about this collection is the kinship Creeley feels with the action painters, who redefined the work of art in terms of its continuity with experience.

Creeley's Olsonian take on Whitman's method as composition by field demonstrates his general attitude. Whitman's poetry does not consist of a series of subjects, "subject" in any case being only one element of composition, but is rather a process coextensive with the poet's life through which his experience is articulated and amplified. So, "it does not talk about or refer to—in the subtlety of its realization, it becomes real." It is not "about" experience, it is an extension of experience. Creeley is not interested in describing anything, he notes in a different essay. Nor in language as the kind of self-contained system (he has the French in mind) that cuts you off from what's happening. Language participates in experience and changes it, and so "it is possible we live entirely in that act we so call 'creative.' "

Language so conceived might argue for a continuity of art and intellect through the idea of the "creative," that theoretically should allow the writer to move from poetics to poetry, and from poetry to prose, depending on the mood and matter at hand, the way a Shakespeare play moves from dialogue to soliloquy, or a Mozart opera from aria to recitative. Creeley allots a tentative preparatory function to his essays as compared to poetry itself, allowing them the place of "invocation." But the invocation is commonly part of the work, is it not? You might say that Creeley and other writers writing on writing offer an informal poetics of composition, as opposed to the more usual scholarly poetics of explication which is of no interest to the writer as writer, though it may be extremely useful to writer as reader. The distinction, though artificial, is necessary in defining each kind of poetics in terms of its area of competence. The art of interpretation has a tendency to usurp that of composition, often giving poetics of any kind a bad name among writers who prefer, in terms of Susan Sontag's distinction, the erotics rather than the hermeneutics of the situation. If, as Renato Poggioli claimed, intellectuals typically reduce art to ideas, then artists value ideas that excite the impulse to generation, to synthesis, to making it, to doing it. Creeley several times alludes to Olson's remark about his desire to "come into" the world. The comparison is acute, in my opinion, though it sounds sloppy. But how much do you get out of being neat? That art is energized more by desire than understanding is something that has to be reckoned with one way or another. And would it not be plausible to argue that the study of composition, as with music, is the best way to move us into intimate and sensuous contact with the text? Henry James' essays on fiction, or Gertrude Stein's, are seminal examples.

Creeley, of course, speaks as a novelist as well as a poet, and similar ideas can be seen in fiction writers as diverse as Richard Brautigan, William Burroughs, George Chambers, and Clarence Major, to name just a few. Which is not to say there are no differences between the genres. Those who are restrictively purist about the novel—harlot of literary forms who think of it as an investigation of language in a continuum with poetry, falsify its nature. But in fact the application of such ideas of composition to fiction since the sixties has had as radical an effect on the novel as it had on poetry considerably earlier, the development of fiction in America having been retarded by the weight of its commercial value. As everyone in his right mind by this time knows, the purpose of form in fiction is not to give an illusion of reality but a sense of artifice, the imprint of a style, the intervention of measure.

Creeley's essays assume a continuity among poetry, fiction, painting, criticism and other arts, and this grasp of context seems to me crucial to the authority the essays convey. And the context Creeley establishes has historical resonance as well, so that you come away from the essays feeling they're plugged into the mainline of American writing. Henry Miller in *Black Spring*, for example, taking off from Whitman to talk about the act of writing as "this expanding moment which has not defined itself in ticks or beats," an act performed by someone existing in time and space whose circumstances enter into the composition: "I notice that when Whitman starts a poem he writes: 'I, Walt, in my 37th year . . .'," an act that does not generate meaning but returns us to its source in experience, the "eternal moment," where there are "no truths to utter," only "a gush and a babble, a speaking to all men at once, everywhere, and in all languages," an act whose thrust is basically erotic, when language, instead of violating your experience, expands it and turns you on to it. Language used in this way does not come to conclusions. There are no conclusions to come to, it just comes.

1981

II. Misreading Bloom

Harold Bloom's *The Poems of Our Climate* (Ithaca: Cornell University Press, 1977) is probably the best book on Stevens, though this isn't high praise. Too quirky to be anything like "definitive," it nevertheless develops a way of considering Stevens's poetry which, seen clear of Bloom's particular critical system and its attendant terminology, should open the way at last for a general assimilation of Stevens's essential importance. Stevens is a psychological poet in the sense that his poems are the record of the movement of a mind. His is not a poetry of thought but of how we think. Its movement is typically from conflict to resolution that breaks down into conflict again. The poet is a man whose mind is never made up: "It can never be satisfied, the mind, never." If Stevens's poems may be said to have a structure, it is fundamentally the structure of the poet's mind as it is realized in the act of improvisation. Hence on the one hand the loose, limitless variations-on-a-theme form, as in "The Man with the Blue Guitar" or "An Ordinary Evening in New Haven," and on the other, the symmetrical but arbitrary forms, as in "Notes toward a Supreme Fiction," which serve as a frame within which to improvise. As opposed to the didactic or philosophic, this poetry's end is not proof but conviction, or persuasion as in rhetoric, except that it is as if Stevens were trying to persuade himself; its goal is not to demonstrate truth but to effect resolution. It does not attempt to assert fact, but rather seeks to adjust belief to fact, to bring about that "agreement with reality believed for a time to be true" that Stevens conceives to be poetic truth. In other words, its area of operation is not that of doctrine, but of psychology. That is why Stevens can write, "It is the belief and not the god that counts," and again, "In the long run the truth does not matter."

Through ingenious use of the terminology peculiar to his cirticism—no matter how tortuous—Bloom captures this basic mode and movement of Stevens's poetry and expounds it with subtle argument, rich detail, and prodigious learning. The greatest contribution of the book is to ground this approach thoroughly in literary tradition and intellectual history. Bloom's reading recognizes and contains the discursive material in the poetry. His Stevens is not a poet of ideas, a philosophical poet. On the contrary, Bloom speaks of "the long tradition of the polemic of philosophy against poetry, in which rhetoric has been at once the fought-over field and the weapons depot for both sides." It is not the epistemological, "concept-thinking" rhetoric of the philosophers through which Stevens can be understood. Rather we must understand Stevens in terms of a persuasive, antithetical rhetoric in the sophistic tradition. Bloom speaks of Gorgias as "a poet leading souls through incantation to the relativity of all truth, and doing this through an antithetical style, one which offered contrasts and alternatives for every definition ventured, in contrast to the Socratic mode of arriving at supposedly absolute truth." This, it seems to me, captures the tone of Stevens precisely. Such a rhetoric is concerned with emotional survival rather than truth, and so Bloom calls for a revivification of "the ancient identity between rhetoric and psychology," whose arena would be the reader's internal discourse, as well as the poet's.

I am, of course, misreading Bloom, and leaving out a great deal of his thesis. But this seems to me what is seminal in his stance with regard to Stevens, from which one might move in many different directions. It should also be noted that, as Denis Donoghue points out in his admirably balanced review in *The New York Review of Books*, the strong focus which Bloom's full critical apparatus provides on some aspects of Stevens's work also inhibits investigation of other aspects which do not happen to be relevant to Bloom's theories. This favors my own sense that Bloom is most useful as a critic if one doesn't take him seriously, a remark which I don't intend to be demeaning. On the contrary, there is an element of play in Bloom's writing which keeps it on the edge of balance and poses a tone of liveliness and surprise against its more ponderous qualities. Bloom's criticism is, like Stevens's poetry, itself the record of a mind in motion. It is an antithetical criticism, sophistic, full of paradox and unexpected turns. It comprises, in fact, what Bloom calls for in the course of his argument, that is, a "diachronic rhetoric." One therefore cannot take any one phase or term in Bloom's evolving theory with absolute seriousness. What Bloom is presenting to us is the intriguing example of a critical intelligence in process of thinking like a poetic intelligence. This makes many critical widows wince. Bloom means to make them wince. He intends to be outrageous and he is. Bloom is a provocateur. He is employing a kind of *patacriticism* to move literary commentary, especially academic literary commentary, out of the realm of systematic "concept-thinking" into that of contingency and the progressive qualification of relativism. There is no such thing as truth. But if there is no such thing as truth, perhaps there is no such thing as theory. In fact, Bloom's purpose is to return criticism from systematic theory to practical criticism. And yet, his own theoretical system is pervasive and heavy-handed and constantly gets in the way of his practical criticism. And yet, if his theory is consistent it should evolve in the direction of self-destruction, theory providing an escape from theory. And yet, Bloom does not mean to be consistent. And yet, and yet, and yet. Which is the point.

As a result of these contradictions, what we are left with in this book is frequently apt theory and frequently inept Stevens explication. When you read Bloom reading Stevens's poems you get Bloom. If you want Bloom it's fine; if you want Stevens, it's not so good. When a poem happens to connect with one of Bloom's abiding concerns the reading is often brilliant, as when he finds an opportunity to establish Stevens firmly in the context of American romanticism. If a poem does not happen to relate to one of those concerns, Bloom misreads it. Or he loses interest. Finally, his reading of Stevens makes one wonder which side, in the battle of philosophy against poetry, Bloom is really on.

1978

III. Gerald Graff

It's provocative to see Gerald Graff in *Literature against Itself* (Chicago: University of Chicago Press, 1979) parallel the theoretical reasoning of people like Northrop Frye, Frank Kermode, and the "radical poststructuralist" critics with that of Mussolini. I used to enjoy reminding "counterculture" pals that Hitler was an artist, a vegetarian, a revolutionary, and a believer in the occult. However, there are many tyrants who eat meat and don't believe in deconstruction. Graff notes that there are arguments coming from the poststructuralists to the effect that it's non-poststructuralists like Graff who tend to authoritarianism. Either way, frankly, the argument seems cheap. It might make more sense, if you were really interested, to see what poetics authoritarian regimes actually encourage.

What's provocative about Graff's linkage of authoritarian politics and current literary theories (the same linkage is sometimes made with innovative fiction) is the fact that he takes those theories so seriously, despite his claim that they're nonsense. The postmodern movement has reduced truth to the status of fiction, he believes, and is partly responsible for the decline of the humanities. Whether you agree with his point of view or not, his book demonstrates that there is political, social, and economic import to the way we use language in its creative and critical forms. And this, in turn, hints at the import of our contemporary literary wars. They concern the nature of "reality," as Graff points out, but that immediately brings up an anterior question: the nature of the authority on which we can make claims about reality. The nature of authority is a question that has political implications, and in literature this is the case whether you're talking about the poetics of the New Criticism or something so practical as the policies of Reagan and Carter regarding the National Endowment for the Arts, where, for example, the authority of elitism versus that of populism has been a very relevant consideration.

Graff likes to turn arguments "on their heads," especially regarding their political implications:

We are inclined to view the relativizing of belief as a liberalizing strategy because it dissolves the authority of dogmatic and totalitarian systems of thought. But this strategy at the same time dissolves the authority of anything that tries to resist these systems, and smooths the moral and psychological paths to mass manipulation.

But very much of what Graff says is reversible. Is it a critical relativism that smooths the path to totalitarianism, or is it, in our society, acceptance of political dogma and consumerist cliché? Is it radical esthetics that encourages a mindless consumer society, or is it that conventional mimetic realism which provides the basis for all those blockbusters in the box office and on the best seller list? Is it really no longer necessary, as it was in the modern period, to "unmask official illusions about the material and moral progress of civilization," or is it even more urgent now that the authorities that promote these illusions "no longer present so clear and visible an ideological target"? Is it "critical permissiveness" to grant the writer his vision, and if so what intellectual commissar will let us know what visions are permissible? Is the "politics of the self" a way of reducing history to psychodrama, or is it a quixotic attempt, in the absence of a viable politics, to salvage individual experience from the assaults of consumerist manipulation? Is it not all the more urgent, given the pressures of that manipulation, to present the reader with a literature that gives him models for a creative truth of "construction" rather than a passive truth of "correspondence," for confrontation and re-creation rather than reconciliation and adjustment through the identification and catharsis inherent in mimetic theory—a Brechtian model rather than an Aristotelian one?

In any case, what is the authority that Graff proposes? He likes to talk about "truth-claims." But in emphasizing the reference of language to factual reality as its claim to truth his book sometime sounds like an apologia for history or journalism rather than an analysis of how we should talk about fiction. To hold fictive language to a standard of truth with reference to empirical reality denies that such language has a reality of its own and that it is a source of knowledge in itself, both in its accumulated wisdom and in its exploration of possibility in the consciously irreal space of fiction. To call the latter kind of truth "mimetic" seems implausible unless you expand the meaning of that term to include all reference in language, which is to reduce it to meaninglessness. Mimetic fiction depends on the suspension of disbelief, nonmimetic fiction does not. By eliminating the need to play let's-pretend, nonimitative art is free to take its part in a serious dialogue with experience, rather than to produce second-hand, platonic "imitations" of "reality." Nonmimetic fiction acknowledges its initial reality as textual, as writing, and in so doing begins by assessing the accuracy and utility of the fictive instrument itself, thus validating itself conditionally as a way of dealing with the subject at hand. In this the truth of fiction is like that provisional truth for which Graff attacks Derrida, of which one can be "skeptical and credulous at the same time." Such fictive truth simultaneously proposes and cancels itself, not to deny the autonomous reality of the world, but to salvage it from the formulations of language. The provisional nature of fictive language allows it both its imaginative freedom and its claim to truth. That "ideal autonomy of poetry," its alienation from social function of which Graff claims postmodern fiction now partakes, has in fact been largely discredited since Olson, Williams, Creeley, the Beats, Abstract Expressionism, and the whole movement of the sixties in fiction, music, and painting. And in this general movement affirmation of the medium has provided an authority for the way out of a modernist hermeticism back into an investigation of common experience.

On the other hand, from a situation of formal self-consciousness leading to a reflexive parody perhaps typified by Barth, Barthelme, Brautigan, and Pynchon, we seem to have moved to a phase of conscious exploration of the many possibilities of the medium. *Literature against Itself* is not a book about fiction but about ways of talking about fiction. When Graff moves from critique of theory to actual consideration of postmodern fiction, his readings are sympathetic to a surprising degree, almost as if he were himself surprised at his approbation. Is it possible that the critics who voice doctrinaire complaints about postmodern fiction haven't read the fiction itself? Early in the book he criticizes Barthelme for "conceding the arbitrary and artificial nature of his creation," without considering the possibility that an acknowledgment of artifice is not necessarily a concession of seriousness. But later on, in a textual analysis, we find him defending Barthelme from supporters and detractors alike as, not surprisingly, the social critic he obviously so often is. Perhaps it is time for American postmodernist and antipostmodernist theoreticians alike to stop using as their battleground traditional texts and a few examples deriving from the sixties, and begin to examine, as their Continental counterparts already have, those contemporary postmodern fictions to which, after all, their theoretical battle might be most appropriate.

1981

IV. Paul Metcalf: The Easy Way Out

Sometimes a writer's strength, though clearly there in his words, does not lie in his apparent intention. Such strength is not a matter of will anyway. Maybe, for example, the power of *Moby-Dick* has more to do with whales and less to do with the mythy material imposed on them than is usually assumed. Maybe the power of Paul Metcalf's *Genoa* has less to do with myth, with schematizations of history, genealogy, Dianetics, and more to do with its method of collage or montage or mosaic that releases it into fascinating material otherwise unavailable in raw form to the novelist. If there's one thing that literature has to do it's to keep escaping literature and this is certainly one way—into the fact of history, of journalism, of recorded myth. And a release of energy follows, the release that always follows the explosion of old form. But the new integration that results is not myth, myth is not something you can invent. It isn't myth but it is new, in fact it's novel. A kind of novel that heads away from suspension of disbelief, which should be reserved for fairytales. Another source of energy in *Genoa* is the way it breaks up the page, thus freeing print for use as an expressive medium, rather than merely a discursive one. There's a lot of Olson in this but no novelist I can think of before, or better than, Metcalf in these precincts. That somewhat similar fictions by the Frenchman, Michel Butor, have been better known in this country than have Metcalf's only indicates that American literati are still snobbish about the native product.

Again in Metcalf's *Patagoni* we get a novel as a concrete artifact like a painting or a sculpture, a worked object in three dimensions. Again we get a collage of fact and experience but what excites me here—what I feel most energy flowing from—is that the experience is direct experience, the author's presumably factual experience interacting with the fact of history, anthropology, and so on. The idea of writing a story that is the record of a trip experienced and invented as one goes along, in the way that one does in fact invent one's experience as one goes along, is an idea that appeals to me enormously. For one thing I like its lack of polish—the opposite of slick. The closer you push to experience the coarser the texture. So here we get a total collage and the fiction is purely in the synthesis. But again the result is not myth but novel. An artist connects the unconnected, myth celebrates connections that are already there. That's one way of putting it. According to Lévi-Strauss the one essential element of myth is that it have no author. That's another way. Or as Wallace Stevens wrote: "Poetry does not address itself to beliefs. Nor could it ever invent an ancient world full of figures that had been known and became endeared to its readers for centuries." Or to put it a final way, art is not a mode of faith, it's a way of thinking. In fact, it's better than thinking because it's easier and more rooted in experience, only we don't have another name for it, a name other than art. Art: the easy way out that's hard to find. Metcalf has found it.

1973

Innovative Fiction/Innovative Criteria

It seems strange to have to talk about innovation in fiction, but the American novel until the end of the sixties was so static that we have not yet fully understood how parochial and narrow the accepted literary norm for fiction had become.

Properly speaking, there is no such thing as "innovative fiction." The novel *is* innovation—it is not called the "novel" for nothing. Fiction is the most fluid and changing of literary forms, the one that most immediately reflects the changes in our collective consciousness, and in fact that is one of its great virtues. As soon as fiction gets frozen into one particular model, it loses that responsiveness to our immediate experience that is its hallmark. It becomes literary. It seems to me that this is one of the major factors contributing to the recent decline in the popularity of fiction: people no longer believe in the novel as a medium that gets at the truth of their lives.

The form of fiction that comes down to us through Jane Austen, George Eliot, and Hemingway is no longer adequate to capture our experience. Either the novel will change, or it will die. Today's money-making novels are those that sell to the movies—in other words, they are essentially written for another medium. No one takes novels seriously until they become movies, which is to say that no one takes novels seriously. Perhaps I exaggerate slightly, but not much. If we are going to have a wide and serious audience for fiction again we are going to have to re-examine the source of the novel's power beyond the particular forms of fiction that have become so dull to so many. And first of all we will have to make a fundamental distinction between fiction and data. The great advantage of fiction over history, journalism, or any other supposedly "factual" kind of writing is that it is an expressive medium. It transmits feeling, energy, excitement. Television can give us the news, but fiction can best express our response to the news. No other medium—especially not film—can so well deal with our strongest and often most intimate responses to the large and small facts of our daily lives. No other medium, in other words, can so well keep track of the reality of our experience. But to do this successfully the novel must continually reinvent itself to remain in touch with the texture of our lives. It must make maximum expressive use of all elements of the printed page, including the relation of print to blank space. It must break through the literary formulas when necessary while at the same time preserving what is essential to fiction: incident, feeling, power, scope, and the sense of consciousness struggling with circumstance.

There is not one new fiction, but many. Novelists today have an unprecedented number of stylistic options, a range of choice involving not so much a struggle of an old form with a new, but an opening out, a broader awareness of the possibilities of the medium. Perhaps the most sensible working definition for what is new in fiction is simply what is not old, what lies outside the literary clichés of the formula of plot, character, and social realism. But this situation also creates problems of judgment: novelty does not guarantee quality, and it becomes crucial to distinguish the superficial from the substantial, regardless of form. To make such distinctions we must go back to the sources of fiction, stripped of inessentials and historical trappings, so that we can recognize the fundamental virtues of the novel though they may appear in odd recombinations and unaccustomed forms. New fiction requires new criteria, but such criteria will be rooted in the essentials of the medium: not plot, but ongoing incident; not characterization, but consciousness struggling with circumstance; not social realism, but a sense of situation; and so on. Innovative fiction, when successful by these criteria, is not "experimental" but represents the progressive struggle of art to rescue the truth of our experience.

1974

Notes

Fiction in the Seventies

1. Morris Dickstein, "Black Humor and History: Fiction in the Sixties," *Partisan Review*, 43, No. 2 (1976), 191.
2. William H. Gass, *Fiction and the Figures of Life* (New York: Alfred A. Knopf, 1970), p. 49.
3. Gass, p. 54.
4. Wallace Stevens, *The Necessary Angel* (New York: Alfred A. Knopf, 1951), p. 8.
5. Michel Foucault, "The Discourse on Language," in *The Archeology of Knowledge*, trans. A. M. Sheridan Smith (New York: Pantheon, 1972), p. 221.
6. Harold Bloom, *The Anxiety of Influence* (New York: Oxford University Press, 1973), pp. 12–13.
7. Frank O'Hara, "Personism: A Manifesto," in Rod Padgett and David Shapiro, eds., *An Anthology of New York Poets* (New York: Vintage Books, 1970), p. xxxiv. (Reprinted from *Yugen*.)
8. Tom Wolfe, "Why They Aren't Writing the Great American Novel Anymore," *Esquire*, 78 (Dec., 1972), p. 272.
9. Richard Pearce, "Enter the Frame," in Raymond Federman, ed., *Surfiction: Fiction Now and Tomorrow* (Chicago: Swallow Press, 1975), p. 56.

10. Raymond Federman, *Take It Or Leave It* (New York: Fiction Collective, 1976).
11. Jean Ricardou, "Writing Between the Lines," in Federman, *Surfiction*, pp. 265–66.
12. George Chambers, *The Bonnyclabber* (Princeton, N.J., and Western Springs, Ill.: Panache and December, 1972), p. 30.

Film Digression

1. William Burroughs, *Le Job, entretiens avec Daniel Odier*, (Paris: Belfond, 1979), pp. 85–86. Quoted in Marc Dachy, *Des Energies transformatrice du langage*, (Paris: FNAGP, 1980), no pagination. Translation mine. Reprinted as *The Job* (New York: Grove Press, 1970), p. 51.

Wallace Stevens: Theory and Practice

1. Frank Kermode, *Wallace Stevens* (Edinburgh and London: Oliver and Boyd, 1960), p. 92. In this regard, one thinks of William Carlos Williams along with Stevens.
2. "Another Way of Looking at the Blackbird," *The New Republic* (Nov. 4, 1957), pp. 17, 18.
3. *Wallace Stevens*, Pamphlets on American Writers, No. 11 (University of Minnesota Press, 1961), p. 29. J. Hillis Miller denies this, as I do, but develops the point differently: "Wallace Stevens' Poetry of Being," in Roy Harvey Pearce and J. Hillis Miller, eds. *The Act of the Mind* (Baltimore: Johns Hopkins University Press, 1965), p. 146. (This article contains the essence of the longer version published in Miller's *Poets of Reality* [Cambridge: Harvard University Press, 1965, pp. 217–284]).
4. For a discussion of Stevens' seasonal cycle, see Kermode, pp. 34–37.
5. Section IX of this poem, however, reaches in the opposite direction, toward order.
6. See Northrop Frye, "The Realistic Oriole," *Hudson Review*, 10 (1957), 363, who comments that Stevens's poetry tries to anni-

hilate "the sense of contrast or great gulf fixed between subject and object, consciousness and existence." N. P. Stallknecht, "Absence in Reality," *Kenyon Review*, 21 (1959), 545, notes that Stevens celebrates the unity of mind and nature as in the Romantic tradition.

7. *Philosophy, The Journal of the British Institute of Philosophy*, 21 (1946), 147–66. Essentially the same statement is found in *NA*, p. 96. See Joseph N. Riddel, "The Authorship of Wallace Stevens' 'On Poetic Truth,' " *MLN*, 76 (1961), 126–29.

8. Abstracted by Stevens from H. D. Lewis' "On Poetic Truth." See n. 7. The passage is exactly apposite to Stevens.

9. "Man Carrying Thing." The same thought with slight variation is found in the "Adagia" (*OP*, p. 171).

10. See Yvor Winters, "The Hedonist's Progress," *In Defense of Reason* (Denver: Alan Swallow, n. d.), pp. 453–54, for a discussion of the history of this distinction in connection with Stevens.

11. Stevens in *Explicator*, 7 (Nov. 1948), Item 18.

12. *Form and Value in Modern Poetry* (Garden City and New York: Doubleday, 1957), p. 222.

13. "Wallace Stevens: The World as Meditation," *Yale Review*, 47 (1958), 517–36.

14. In terms of his theory Stevens uses abstraction to mean "a quality of being taken out, abstracted in the root sense" (Martz, "The World as Meditation," p. 531); "artificial in its proper sense, something constructed rather than generalized" (Frye, "Realistic Oriole," p. 365). An abstraction in this sense is an artificial construction of elements selected from reality.

15. Stevens uses the phrase in relation to section XX.

16. The attempt to define this experience was suggested by J. V. Cunningham, who took note of it in "Tradition and Modernity: Wallace Stevens" (formerly published in *Poetry*, 75 [1949], 149–65), *Tradition and Poetic Structure* (Denver: Alan Swallow, 1960), pp. 122–23.

17. See Miller "Wallace Stevens' Poetry of Being," pp. 157–61, for a discussion of Stevens's perception of being.

18. For an account of the dynamic relation between these two terms of the experience, see above, "Ego and Reality."